DANCING
WITH
TIGERS

DANCING
WITH
TIGERS

Janet E. Lapp, PhD

Demeter Press
San Diego
California

Demeter Press
P.O.Box 124920
San Diego, California 92101

LC: 94-96110
ISBN: 1-885365-01-2

Manufactured in the United States of America
First Printing: March 1994

DEDICATION

To my mother,
with my deepest love.

For your courage,
your strength,
and your chicken paprika.

ACKNOWLEDGMENT

To Carolyn Reid, my copy editor, friend, and daughter,
for your insight, guidance, encouragement
and support through every step of this manuscript.
Your courage to dance with your own tigers
has blessed my journey, and made the travel easier.

To others on my path who have taught me:
My daughter Susan, my dad, Christopher, McGoo,
Andreé, Ted, and Rev. Kathy Hearn. Thank you.

CONTENTS

DANCING
WITH
TIGERS

DANCING WITH TIGERS

I have no idea of the size of this zoo. I lie on the cool floor, with memories of the Danii plains, of my frolicking cubhood, of the deep rain forests.

If you could read my thoughts, you would slip your arm through the bars, and I would hold out my forepaw to greet you. Instead, you recoil because my claws and fangs and glowing eyes frighten you.

Let me tell you my story. At the far end of the Danii range, I lived with my mother in my cave on the edge of a little river which roared during the rainy season. One night, my mother disappeared from my world. Seized with panic, I hid myself in the cave. When I finally ventured out, I was chased, knocked down, and hurt by bigger animals, and threatened by smaller ones.

In the course of time, I learned to fight so well that I considered myself the Lord of the Jungle, striking terror in the hearts of every creature in my path. Half-sunk in jungle grass, I prowled through the plains, creatures shuddering and withdrawing from my path. Such attention pleased me. Among our jungle community, we had an understanding of my undisputed superiority.

One day, beyond the eucalyptus groves, I encountered a creature sitting erect in the middle of the road,

11

blocking my passage. My temper rose at the sight of her. "Get out of my way," I roared. She showed no response except a slight wave of her tail. Furious, I jumped on her back, my claws buried in her skin, and she gashed my eyes and bit my throat. We butted, scratched, clawed, and tore into each other, until we both lay bloodied and near death.

Out of the forest appeared a hyena, who had been attentive to our encounter. "If you have any good reason why you fought, I will spare you." Neither the creature nor I could think of a single good reason. But the hyena was gracious. "Would it not make more sense if you worked together and helped each other? What a formidable force then you would be!" And the hyena turned on her heels and was gone.

With whatever strength was spared us, we nursed each other's wounds, clambered to our feet, and walked in pace with each other. As we regained our strength, the pace quickened, and our movements became rhythmic and musical. From a distance, the hyena and other forest creatures swore that we were dancing.

Now, years later, my dancing years long gone and my capture only a fleeting memory, I lie here alone, urging you to reach your hand through the bars for me. *I* am not fear. The fear is within you. If you would only reach out to me, touch me, you and I could still dance a wonderful dance. Come, embrace me.

PREFACE

Our tiger represents that instinctual and courageous part of us that, when injured, either aggresses or withdraws. When we are given the gifts of feared creatures on our path, and choose to confront and embrace those creatures, not only do we become whole, we incorporate the energy of the feared objects. We then can choose to move to higher levels. In this story, we are at once the tiger and the creature.

If we scatter from our own fear, as the jungle creatures scatter from the tiger, fear roams unchallenged in our lives and dominates us. Once we stand firm, stand still, we harness the energy once contained in our fear. The secret is not in dominating, controlling or conquering fear. It's in using fear as an ally, a friend, a messenger on our path, who has energy to give us, is part of our journey, and who would help us if we would but stand still long enough to let it.

"It is not that you must be free from fear.
The moment you try to free yourself from fear,
you create a resistance against fear.
What is needed, rather than running away or controlling
or suppressing or any other resistance, is understanding fear;
that means, watch it, learn from it, come directly into
contact with it. We are to learn about fear, not how to
escape from it, not how to resist it through courage
and so on." Krishnamurti

DANCING WITH TIGERS

My journey has taken me through several paths of fear. I thought that if I just knew more, or practiced the healing arts enough, that I too would be healed from fear. My knowledge gathering was both my protection and my defense. My healing began not with knowledge, however, but with inspirational stories, the love of my children, with honesty, and with letting go, guided by the healing souls placed on my path.

One of the most difficult blocks in my path was my belief that since I had inherited what they termed 'bad blood' from my manic-depressive father, that I was predestined to just cope with my lot. For many years I was "just the way I was" and I had best learn to accept whatever was this "defective thing." I never saw my "symptoms" as my "strengths." Above all, this 'something wrong' was shameful, and needed to be covered up, if not from myself, then at least from others who could discover my weaknesses.

If dysfunction is in your past—if you have come from a painful place—this place represents the healthiest part of you which was simply acting to resist an unhealthy system. The stronger our resistance, that is, development of our symptoms, the stronger we are, and the greater our calling or potential as a healer. Our 'symptoms' are our calling. Just as Einstein showed learning problems, and Churchill extreme shyness, our weaknesses are strengths in training. When I began to refocus my symptoms as strengths, then my healing began.

DANCING WITH TIGERS

I began this book armed with academic research on risk-taking theory, step-by-step methods to calculate risk potential, and clinical and organizational strategies for intelligent risk-taking. It becamse clear after many months that it was not what wanted to be written. It didn't speak to what I believe is our real need; to be able to reinterpret our weaknesses as strengths, to overcome our collective victim mentality, and to go forward into these confusing times filled with faith, not fear.

In this book I share some lessons, stories and quotes that have helped me on my path. I write in simple words, because that is how I feel. I believe that what is most worthwhile in life may not be able to be supported empirically, can't be discussed by the head, but must be felt by the heart.

I hope that my work serves to guide you on your journey, and that you enjoy your trip.

Janet Lapp

San Diego, California
March, 1994

INTRODUCTION

"We are what we think. All that we are arises with our thoughts, and with our thoughts we make our world."
Buddhist saying.

When we begin to heal, our emotions emerge at random times. If you are feeling new emotions now, or different emotions, it's because these are the ones you should have felt as a child but couldn't because they were too strong or confusing. You won't feel your emotions this strongly forever, just long enough to work them through. The presence of emotions is a good sign, especially anger and sadness. They will pass when they no longer serve you.

We re-create our past until the patterns are conscious and solved. We choose people unconsciously with which to work out these patterns, and we act in ways to confirm the patterns. What is repeated from childhood is the pattern and the emotional reaction, not the external players. Habits are changed slowly, starting with the least threatening (and therefore most available) situations. That's why we might find it easier to be assertive at work than we do with our families. We work around the edges of the target, and move toward the bull's-eye. We can score around the edges of the target and get proficient there, then slowly move in toward the center where it's more difficult.

Change is always awkward. When we are saying and doing things for the first time, we'll be awkward and feel embarrassed. It's a good sign that we're able to do this, because those people who cannot tolerate that embarrassment find it very hard to change.

CHOICE

Once we accept that life is so because *we* have chosen it to be that way—even if the choices were made when we didn't know of any other options—then changing is easier. As long as I perceive others to be responsible for my life and demand that they meet my needs, I can't accept that the choices were mine, and thus I can't change the choices. Each of the major world religions reflect the truth that the choice lies within us.

From Confucianism:
What the undeveloped man seeks is outside; what the advanced man seeks is within himself.

From Buddhism:
If you think the Law is outside yourself, you are embracing not the absolute Law but some inferior teaching.

From Shintoism:
*Do not search in distant skies for God.
In man's own heart is He found.*

From Hinduism:
God bides hidden in the hearts of all.

If we don't make the choices we need to make, and give others responsibility for our lives and actions, we feel immediate resentment for them. Resentment is caused by giving control of our lives to someone else. By not speaking up, not making our own choices, and not stopping abusive situations, we are living out an archaic, primitive dream that we must be completely cared for, and if people don't care to the degree that we demand that they care (which they can't), we must be enraged with them.

Resentment will kill over time, taking our energy first, making our life an emotional roller coaster, then weakening our immune system. At each moment of resentment, we are geared up to take "revenge" but we fail to take action. Chemicals are being secreted in response to our resentment or feelings of revenge. Because our physical system doesn't take action, the chemicals just circulate around our body, wearing out our immune system.

If we've chosen to be in a powerless state, we become driven by anger and resentment. We play our game of sacrifice, our victim game, and hope that it will create of us a hero or that God will smile in a final favor on judgment day. The best we get with this is an unhappy life and the worst is that we bore God.

Being miserable and angry is hard work. Reacting, complaining, feeling that "it's not fair," moaning about what "they're doing to us" takes our energy away. When you are ready, be done with it. There's too much work to be done. The world needs your energy.

DANCING WITH TIGERS

Just as important, when we're in misery and anger, we secrete "toxic hormones" to others, and drive them away. You can't see these hormones. In an experiment at Stanford University, researchers caused a fear reaction in rats. They then removed the rats from the lab and brought in other rats with no previous exposure. As soon as the new group of rats entered the room, they developed a fright reaction even before the experiment began. Why? The experimenters reasoned that they had picked up "fear hormones" from the previous rats. We can't block these hormonal responses with forced smiles and a cheery appearance. In order to really connect with others, we need to make the choice to let resentment go.

HEROES

Heroes emerge at times of dying; the death of the self, of social sanctions, of governments, of relationships. When the call is answered, heroes discover the courage to undergo the gestations,growth,and trauma needed for a new birth. This happens so they can serve as midwives in the larger society to bring themselves and others to a higher level of being. The soul is where the roles of the hero and heroine are considered heroes.

"The challenges of our times are no more over-whelming than the challenges of any other time. The problems lie not in the size of our challenges but in the size of our consciousness. We must change. Change is simply the flow of life. We must let go of our heroes and find the hero within ourselves." Norman Schwarzkof

In becoming a hero or heroine, we withdraw from every day life and open ourselves to the zones wherein lie our means of reaching our spiritual source. The second job that heroes or heroines have is to return to the ordinary life bearing the knowledge they have gained in their work in the depths, and put it to good use to redeem time and society. The patients I have had all represent potential heroes and heroines, and as they "return to the world," they embark on their own healing missions.

DANCING WITH TIGERS

Ram Dass, in *Journey of Awakening,* describes the hero's journey as a mountain climb:

"Picture a beautiful warm summer day. A group of people has decided to climb a nearby mountain. The going is easy, the day gentle. After several hours they reach a plateau with a rest station. Here they find a restaurant comfortable chairs, rest rooms, telescopes—all the conveniences. The view is inspiring. The air cooler and clearer than down below. A sense of well-being, of health and energy, animates the climbers body and soul. For many in the group, this is enough. Many return home feeling refreshed and satisfied. They are called day climbers.

A few remain, having discovered another path. Perhaps it is the same path that began far down the valley. Impelled by the need to explore, they start forward onto it. After a while the air grows cooler still. The trees thin out. Clouds obscure the view from time to time. The path keeps rising, getting steeper and steeper. It is not yet beyond the skill of those who are determined to go on.

They reach a second rest area, with no conveniences other than an outhouse and an outdoor fireplace. The comraderie is now deeper. Their eyes feast a grander view. The villages in which they grew up lie tiny and remote from this new distance. It is their past they see in a new perspective. They see the limits of their lives in the valley far below. Few people leave this station to travel higher. Most stay for awhile, then go back down.

DANCING WITH TIGERS

Some remain—a handful. They seek and find a hidden path disappearing above. Are they ready to ascend the flat faces of rocks, to creep along narrow ledges, to explore caves high above, to crawl up to the snow line and beyond? They feel some fear and loneliness now, some confusion. They ask themselves why they left the conviviality of the rest stop to tackle this painful, dangerous journey—or is it a pilgrimage? Their physical hardships reflect their spiritual struggle. The obstacles of rock and cliff mirror the possibility of great injury, worse than before because the openness and risk are greater.

Added now is an inner battle. The climbers feel they have taken on an adversary. The mountain has become something to be mastered and controlled. Of the handful of people that climbs to this height, only one or two can reach the top. Those few who go for broke, who want to reach the top, will use their every tool to its utmost. They want all of it, the top of the mountain, the mystic experience every great climber has known. After one arrives at the summit, after going through the total transformation of being, after becoming free of fear, doubt, confusion, and self-consciousness, there is yet one more step to the completion of that journey: the return to the valley below, to the every day world.

Who it is that returns is not who began the climb in the first place. The being that comes back is quietness itself, is compassion and wisdom, is the truth of the ages. Whatever humble or elevated position that being holds within the community, he or she be comes a light for others on the way, a statement of the freedom that comes from having touched the top of the mountain. The return completes the cycle. It is this cycle which brings the spirit to earth and allows the divine to feed once again the hopes and aspirations, the barely sensed possibility, that exists in each human being."

Each of us becomes a potential hero at any point where we choose the higher path, make the more difficult journey, or make the decision to act or think in a healthier way. We *become* heroes by staying the path, by forging through the fears, doubts, and self-imposed limitations that threaten us at every turn. Heroes aren't necessarily those who've captured the attention and imagination of the world. Those heroes are often just the projections of wishes and dreams by a society who has a glorified but limited notion of "hero."

Real heroes undergo tremendous personal journeys, gather their healing strength from within on the trip, and quietly emerge at the top. When they do, their healing work in the world, just as quietly, begins.

HEALTHY IN UNHEALTHY PLACES

Sigmund Freud once explained that the place where a crystal is broken is the place that most clearly reveals its structure. We can discover its nature by examining where it is cracked. In the same way, our own pain can be the path to explore our own essence, revealing the depth of truth within us, if only we would sit with the silence and give up our chatter of blame.

Adults who were hurt as children show inner wisdom, creativity and insight. Within them early on, was the deepest knowledge that life was good, abundant and joyful. Not experiencing that in childhood, they have spent much of their lives in search of the peace they just imagined in childhood.

A painful childhood helps us focus attention on the inner life and heightens our awareness. For safety, we learned to watch more closely, listen more carefully, attend to the subtle imbalances around us. We learned to feel the feelings of others, attend to every conflict, every piece of information that may could hold some protection or some teaching for us. Seen this way, family trauma isn't a defect to be healed or a disease to be cured, but a potent inner strength that becomes a midwife to a more powerful experience.

Paradoxically, a painful childhood can be a gift. What we felt then and what we have had to re-experience and grow through didn't always seem like a gift. Yet through this pain, we learned an intuition, sensitivity, and a devotion to healing. These are gifts to be valued and nurtured.

We're not broken; we're not irrevocably shaped. We don't need to repair anything. All we need to do is to reawaken what is already wise, strong, and whole within us, to allow those qualities of heart and spirit that are in us to break through our shell.

> "Your life is not a problem to be solved
> but a gift to be opened."
>
> Wayne Muller in *Legacy of the Heart.*

Any child who is emotionally hurt will seek the comfort of parents. Yet some families, through denial or inattention, won't be able to feel the hurt, or will need to minimize or deny it. When our parents ignored or discounted our pain, there was no name for the feeling. For that reason, we redoubled the effort to name the suffering and to find the truth about it. Thus, in addition to the initial pain, we added anger, confusion, or shame.

Too, children carry the unexpressed emotion of the family; some carry anger, some sadness, some fear, some happiness; whichever emotion can't or won't be expressed by the family. For example, if our parents didn't express anger, we'll carry the emotion for them. Nature requires a balance and requires expression. When we work through and understand whose emotions are whose, we may be able to let some of the troubling 'carried' emotions go. We no longer need to carry *their* feelings for *them*; that's *their* job. They're adults—let them express their own feelings and do their own work. We have enough work of our own to do.

It's natural to attach to our pain and suffering with anger or shame. Anger and shame are very powerful ways of hanging on. Because our pain is all that we knew *then,* we're afraid to let go of the attached resentment, shame, anger, or fear *now* because it is all that we still know. If we give it up we won't have *anything.* But those emotions no longer serve us and keep us trapped. Memories of hurts can become so strong that they colour our whole lives, and we seek nothing but to rectify the damage done to us. By seeing our pain as damage, we seek restitution. By seeing our hurt as *strength*, we can give ourselves permission to nourish it, care for it, and heal it—and in so doing—heal ourselves.

Some think that we become aware of our potential greatness at birth, and as we grow, being aware of our destiny, we develop symptoms that make sense given what we perceive to be this great and frightful future ahead of us. The symptoms are preparing us by making us stronger, and portend our future. I wonder what would happen if we began to wonder not how our symptoms cripple us, but what message do, and did, they hold for us? Symptoms may show strength, not weakness. For example, depression slows us down so that we can be in a place where deeper messages can reach us. Only if we stop our self-blame, and accept our symptoms as strengths, can we let the messages in.

DARK NIGHTS

*"In the middle of the journey of our life,
I came to myself in a dark wood."*
Dante in the *Divine Comedy*

As one climber of the Aconcagua mountain said after successfully reaching the top, "For the ordeal I had just undergone, joy might seem an odd description. But that is what I felt: the joy of accomplishment, of having been tested—the joy of being alive. The cares and complications of my life had receded into the valley."

"Only by contact with evil could I have learned to feel by contrast the beauty of truth and love and goodness."
Helen Keller

We all want instant decisions and snap answers, while the truest answers emerge quietly only during the deepest part of the journey. The British decreed that Indians had to buy salt from the English so that they may profit, but they were prohibited from using the plentiful supply on the beach. Ghandi went into retreat to ponder the issue, and at the end of a month, emerged with an idea. In pure simplicity, he decided to journey to the sea to pick up a handful of salt. He walked across India, the news media in tow, and after many days he finally reached the shore, stooped over, and in picking up one handful of salt, the British Empire's domination of India crumbled. Ghandi's growth and illumination developed during his dark times, alone, when he withdrew from society.

27

DANCING WITH TIGERS

Each growth journey demands a detribalization, or withdrawal from society. If you have already been labeled, or ostracized, or hospitalized in a psychiatric facility, you have already "served your first time." As a sane child in an insane place, or as one such labeled, you have already stepped outside your culture's limiting and distorting beliefs. By developing "symptoms" you have already removed yourself from your family of origin and stepped outside the "idols of the marketplace" as Francis Bacon terms them. You have already done much of your work in this world. Congratulations.

All growth requires periodic disengagement from culture, requires solitude, or requires immersion in another culture or within detribalized people. As author Arnold Toynbee looked back over cultures, he discovered one common characteristic: those who contributed most to their cultures all showed the cycle of withdrawal and return to society. The withdrawal process from our usual life is for a period of reflection, to plumb own very depths for answers. Having found the source, we return to the world to share.

DANCING WITH TIGERS

Instead of pushing yourself to change, draw yourself into the future. Imagine you are in the world a few years in the future, having made the contributions you'd like to make. Where are you? How do you feel? What is the setting? What is your body posture?

Answer these questions:
What is your *life* teaching other people?

What is the contribution you've made to the world
for which you feel most proud?
What other contributions have you made?

To make this contribution to the world, in what way would
you have to stop underestimating yourself?
To make this contribution to the world, in what way would
you have to stop underestimating other people?

What strengths or capacities would you
have to recognize in yourself?
What strengths or capacities would you
have to recognize in others?
What would you have to stop pretending that you can't do?

What would you have to recognize
as really important to you?
What would you have to recognize
as something very unimportant to you?

What could you do right now to begin making this
contribution? If it feels right, do it.

29

WORTH

The universe is designed to express something through each of us, or we wouldn't have been born. There was a space created in the universe for each of us at the moment of our birth. Whatever we are meant to express, we do so through *attention*. It's the sustained, devoted attention we give to whatever it is that we have decided to do, that allows its expression. It doesn't matter to *what* we pay attention, as long as it is in line with what we feel in our hearts is right for us, and what we truly enjoy.

What is meant to be expressed? In the movie Karate Kid, Miaga was teaching the Karate Kid how to trim a Bonsai. His advice? "Never try to do it. Picture it, then turn around." "How do I know when it's right?" the Karate Kid asked. Miaga responded: "The answer will come from inside you. Trust it."

It's not our job to judge the worth of what we do, because that something in the universe that can be expressed only through us simply needs to be expressed, and we are doing our spiritual work. The Lord won't ask us why we didn't write that best-selling novel, or find the cure for cancer, or fit into a size 4 dress, but she will ask if we let the energy from that unique us come out. By judging what we do, questioning what we know, doubting what we believe ... we limit ourselves. The imperfect real self is what lets truth in, that is, the universe responds only when we're not blocking its energy with our self-doubts.

DANCING WITH TIGERS

"There is a vitality, a life-force, an energy, a quickening that
is translated through you into action. And because there is
only one you in all of time, this expression is unique.
And if you block it, it will never exist through any other
medium and be lost. The world will not have it.
It is not your business to determine how good it is nor how
valuable nor how it compares with other expressions.
It's your business to keep it yours clearly and directly,
to keep the channel open ... whether you choose to take an
art class, keep a journal, record your dreams, dance your
story or live each day from your own creative source.
Above all else, keep the channel open."

Choreographer Martha Graham

DANCING WITH TIGERS

As songwriter Leonard Cohen says: "Forget your perfect offering. There's a crack in everything. That's how the light gets in." Our perfection is in our 'human-ness.'

The birds they sang at the break of day
Start again I heard them say
Dont dwell on what has passed away.
Or what is yet to be.

The wars they will be fought again.
The holy dove be caught again
bought and sold and bought again.
The dove is never free.

Ring the bells that still can ring
Forget your perfect offering.
There is a crack in everything.
That's how the light gets in.

ANTHEM © 1992 Leonard Cohen Stranger Music Inc.

DANCING WITH TIGERS

A jug maker found a pumpkin vine with a tiny pumpkin on it that had just begun to grow. Out of curiosity, he slipped the pumpkin inside one of his jugs and left it. When harvest time came, he found the pumpkin had grown only as large as the confines of the jug. The pumpkin's potential and form had been limited and shaped by the jug. How successful can you become? If you reached out, broke your jug, I wonder what you could become? What are your judgments and beliefs about your potential or who you are? These "thought jugs" serve you to keep you safe, and once served you well. If they no longer serve you, question whether or not you will keep them. Your beliefs and rules are meant to serve you, not the other way around.

The Buddha tells this story:

A young widower, who loved his five-year-old son very much, was away on business, and bandits came, burned down his whole village, and took his son away. When the man returned, he saw the ruins and panicked. He took the charred corpse of an infant to be his own child, and he began to pull his hair and beat his chest, crying uncontrollably. He organized a cremation ceremony, collected the ashes, and put them in a very beautiful velvet pouch. Working, sleeping, or eating, he always carried the bag of ashes with him.

One day his real son escaped from the robbers and found his way home. He arrived at his father's new cottage at midnight, and knocked at the door. You can imagine, at that time, the young father was still carrying the bag of

33

ashes, and crying. He asked, "Who is there?" And the child answered, "It's me, Papa. Open the door, it's your son." In his agitated state of mind the father thought that some mischievous boy was making fun of him, and he shouted at the child to go away, and continued to cry. The boy knocked again and again, but the father refused to let him in. Some time passed, and finally the child left. From that time on, father and son never saw one another.

After telling this story, the Buddha said, "Sometime, somewhere you take something to be the truth. If you cling to it so much, when the truth comes in person and knocks on your door, you will not open it."

What we have collected in our lives so far is a direct result of our consciousness, what we feel we are worth. As soon as we stop looking for what we want and become what we want to attract in our lives, it shows up. "What kind of person must I become to attract to me what I deserve ? What consciousness do I need?"

Each of us is surrounded by an invisible "Circle of Availability" that we've developed based on beliefs of scarcity, lack, or diminished self-worth. Whatever we believe is in this circle is available to us; whatever is outside, we believe is available to others but not to us.

It might make sense now to take a pencil and draw a circle. Write inside the circle what you have presently, and write outside the circle those things you want, but feel you can't get, or don't deserve. For each of the items inside the circle, ask yourself: Is this truly what I want, and, supposing

DANCING WITH TIGERS

I were worth as much as anyone else, that I deserve? If yes, keep it. If no, work on removing it. For each of the items outside the circle ask: What stops me from deserving this? What fear do I have to overcome in order to place it inside?

When what we want lies outside the circle, what typically binds us is fear, or rather our fear of fear. Many people organize their lives so that they never venture outside their Circle and so avoid confronting their fears. Our circles are expanded by our belief that we are worth whatever the universe has to offer, by learning that whatever we need is already inside the circle if we choose to open our eyes to it. By judging what we do, questioning what we know, doubting what we believe—we limit ourselves.

If our circle is small, and we want more, typically we'll work on *getting* more. Ironically, our circles are expanded not by getting more, but by *giving* more. Giving expands our circle, because in giving, we're acknowledging that we *have enough*. And the acknowledgement of *having enough* indicates our self-worth. Whatever we need is already inside the circle.

Divine Master, grant that I may not
so much seek to be consoled, as to console;
to be understood, as to understand;
to be loved, as to love;
for it is in giving that we receive;
it is in pardoning that we are pardoned;
and it is in dying that we are born to eternal life.

Francis of Assisi

DANCING WITH TIGERS

If our lives aren't abundant in any area, it's because we're holding both arms up to the source, blocking it from us. As Jack Canfield has said: "We get in the way of our own magnificence."

"If you deliberately plan to be less than you are capable of becoming, then I warn you that you'll be deeply unhappy for the rest of your life. You will be evading your own capacities, your own responsibilities." Abraham Maslow

If we believe that we do nothing that changes the world consider this:

"Every good thing you do, every good thing you say, every good thought you think, vibrates on and on and never ceases. The evil remains only until it is overcome by the good, but the good remains forever." Peace Pilgrim

It takes only one person. Leadership doesn't need to come from management. Heroes emerge from acts of ordinary people. Each time one of us takes a difficult inward journey, civilization is moved forward as much or more than with an outward journey. When God has healing work to be done on earth, she sends heroes to the earth who dare to be healed, who are brave enough to travel that inward journey. It may be our mission in this life to take the inner journey, knowing that in so doing, we're changing the world in a deeply significant way.

DANCING WITH TIGERS

When a seed germinates, it first sends a root downward into the earth. Only when the root is firmly established, do limbs and branches begin to form. When constructing a skyscraper that will tower hundreds of feet in the air, builders first dig into the ground. Only when the foundation is complete does upward construction begin. We are doing important work in the world even if there appears to be no outward manifestation of it. If we are doing interior healing, then we are doing useful work.

The courageous acts of ordinary people changing the world... A black woman named Rosa Parks refusing to sit at the back of the bus. A migrant worker called Cesar Chavez demanding that the immigrant workers be paid a living wage. Keith Meinhold, a gay naval officer telling his story to the joint chiefs as they deliberate lifting the ban. Rosa Parks, Cesar Chavez, and Keith Meinhold never realized what their acts of courage would achieve, but today we live in a better world because of them. If you believe that there's nothing you can do as one person to change the world, remember these ordinary people who were simply following their beliefs.

Each person counts, as we're *giving* or being *given to*. In the words of Mother Theresa: "I never look at the masses as my responsibility. I look at the individual. I can love only one person at a time. I can feed only one person at a time. Just one, one, one.... So you begin–I begin. I picked up one person—maybe if I didn't pick up that one person I wouldn't have picked up 42,000. The whole work is only a drop in the ocean. But if I didn't put the drop in, the ocean would be one drop less. Same thing for you, same thing in your family, same thing in the church where you go. Just begin . . . one, one, one."

"If you are faced with a challenge, refuse to be panic-stricken. Life has not ended for you. Life flows on. Declare for yourself: I accept the reality of this situation, but not its permanence."

Eric Butterworth

When we come to the last moment of this lifetime, and we look back across it, the only thing that's going to matter is "What was the quality of our love?"

Richard Bach

Our first duty is not to hate ourselves.

Swami Vivekananda

"God regards with merciful eyes not what you are nor what you have been but what you wish to be."

The Cloud of Unknowing

"When I have forgiven myself and remembered who I am, I will bless everyone and everything I see."

A Course in Miracles

HAPPINESS

Happiness doesn't just occur by good luck, and we can't be happy by setting out to find it. The philosopher John Stuart Mill, once said, "Ask yourself whether you are happy, and you cease to be so." Happiness is a by-product of a well-lived life, of being fully involved with each detail of our lives, whether good or bad.

Viktor Frankl, in *Man's Search for Meaning* said, "Do not aim at success—the more you aim at it and make it a target the more you are going to miss it. For success, like happiness, cannot be pursued, it must ensue … as the unintended side effect of one's personal dedication to a course greater than oneself." The course greater than oneself can be the active pursuit of any worthwhile activity or goal that lies just beyond our grasp; one for which we must push ourselves to reach. Mihaly Csikszentmihalyi has called this the experience of "flow."

If you've sensed a zest for life or a feeling of aliveness in some people, it probably comes from the spaces just outside their Circle of Availability or comfort zone, of the places where they are living in their danger zones. All creativity, change, and growth happens outside the circle, and it's this zone alone that brings the exhilaration. Someone once said that "the periods of exhilaration in life happen when our bodies or minds are stretched to their limits in a voluntary effort to accomplish something difficult and worthwhile." They come when we are active in life, by our

39

choice, in the pursuit of something. They do not happen while we are sitting around waiting for them to happen. Where you feel most alive is usually not where you feel most safe or comfortable.

These feeling-good times, or "optimal experiences," lead to a sense of mastery, a sense of participation in the content of our lives—and are about as close as we can get to happiness. When a pianist masters a complicated passage, or a climber reaches the top of a mountain, or a person loses weight, the pain of the process passes and the exhilaration follows. All the years of agony and pain are worth the one moment of sheer ecstasy you feel when you finally get it. That moment has an automatic erase on it; you don't feel the pain *or* the fear, only the exhilaration. Then you get to move to a higher level.

Csikszentmihalyi in *Flow: The Psychology of Optimal Experience*, states that activities that give us the most satisfaction in life are those that engage our psychic energy in increasingly complex and challenging tasks— whether mountain climbing, reading, painting, meditating, solving a complicated business problem, or performing a flawless figure skating program. When we are in "flow," the activity absorbs the body and mind. We lose our "self," and order and harmony prevail. Most flow experiences happen while people are working—meeting new challenges that match their skills and interests. Yet, popular culture values leisure over work.

DANCING WITH TIGERS

For example, people watch television when they don't enjoy it very much because it requires no effort. Playing the piano or taking a bike ride are much more enjoyable, but take greater expenditures of psychic and physical energy. So, we save a small amount of energy up front by watching television, but we forfeit the opportunity to experience flow, and to grow in complexity when we do so. While watching television may be entertaining, it fails to challenge the mind and increase complexity. In a more recent book, *The Evolving Self,* Csikszentmihalyi proposes that *flow experiences* lead to the "increased complexity in consciousness" that's needed to evolve the self. This "complexity" also provides the energy and direction for some of the most important transformations of culture. Thus, simply by stretching ourselves, we help transform society to a higher place.

It doesn't really matter what we do, or in which area of life we concentrate. All activities that challenge us to operate outside our comfort zone will bring the same satisfaction. Many of us scatter around from one activity to the next, searching for satisfaction, not knowing that there are infinite levels of discovery in *each person*, in *each thing* we do. When we move too fast, we never discover these. If we run away at the sign of the first block, or frustration, the deepest we get in life is to the first block of a bunch of unsatisfying activities or relationships. As we remove the blocks and start working at deeper levels, we discover these infinite levels. Move beyond the blocks. Thankfully, they're all within ourselves, not *out there*.

41

DANCING WITH TIGERS

"A young lad was sent to school. He began his lessons with the other children, and the first lesson the teacher set him was the straight line, the figure "one." But whereas the others went on progressing, this child continued writing the same figure. After two or three days the teacher came up to hm and said, "Have you finished your lesson?" He said, "No, I'm still writing 'one.' " He went on doing the same thing, and when at the end of the week the teacher asked him again he said, "I have not yet finished it."

The teacher thought he was an idiot and should be sent away, as he could not or did not want to learn. At home the child continued with the same exercise and the parents also became tired and disgusted. He simply said, "I have not yet learned it, I am learning it. When I have finished I shall take the other lessons." The parents said, "The other chldren are going on further, school has given you up, and you do not show any progress; we are tired of you."

And the lad thought with sad heart that as he had displeased his parents too he had better leave home. So he went into the wilderness and lived on fruits and nuts. After a long time, he returned to his old school. And when he saw the teacher he said to him, "I think I have learned it. See if I have. Shall I write on this wall?" And when he made his sign the wall split in two."

Hazrat Inayat Khan
The Sufi Message of Hazrat Inayat Khan

DANCING WITH TIGERS

Every time we undertake and complete something that was hard for us, our self-esteem grows. But strength doesn't grow on completion, it grows in the spaces between the actions we take to finish something. The steps are only external manifestations of the growing strength. The real rewards lie in what happens in between. Completing gives a sense of pride, but it's in the striving that self-esteem grows the most. The more we actively engage in challenge the more we realize that we have the potential to emerge a stronger person.

Wishing doesn't complete—many of us spend our lives wishing. We can read, watch TV, rent videos and we'll learn how others live their lives but we won't be building our own lives, and so we'll always feel a sense of emptiness, a lack, a yearning for something deeper.

As we strive, we begin to see ourselves as resourceful, capable, and resilient. We'll find ourselves redefining our relationships, behaving more assertively, becoming less willing to tolerate people who are energy drainers. Because our self-esteem doesn't depend on other people's approval, we're more free to choose people to be around us with whom we can be completely ourselves.

BE WHERE YOU ARE

From Jane Wagner's play "In Search for Intelligent Signs of Life in the Universe," Lily Tomlin in the role of Trudy the Bag Lady says it well: "When I was little I always knew that when I grew up, I wanted to be somebody. Now I wish I'd been more specific." When who we are isn't given clear voice, the best we can do is to wish we were something else. Usually anything that we aren't.

When we're always trying to be where we are not, we're never where we are, and so what we have is never good enough, only what we don't have. A juniper can spend a lifetime stretching up to become a redwood, and in the end, becomes only a depressed, stunted juniper. If we spend our lives complaining about the hand dealt to us, we can't play the cards in our hand. How can we possibly win? As long as our core belief is that we are defective the way we are now, we won't have the psychic energy to change the things that we really could change.

By judging what we do, questioning what we know, doubting what we believe—we cancel ourselves and block the life energy that has to come out through us. Don't look around for the right thing to do. There isn't a right thing to do. Whatever comes up for us is the right thing to do right then. We already have the skill and knowledge we need for anything we choose to do. Otherwise we wouldn't have chosen it. If it comes into our consciousness, it is essentially already done. It just needs attention to give it form.

DANCING WITH TIGERS

If people judge us, limit us, and define us, they are projecting their own limitations onto us, and using us to judge themselves. Run for cover. Let's choose only healthy people who accept us the way we are. We do not overreact. We are not too sensitive. We are not too emotional. It's fundamentally impossible. Whatever comes up in us is a natural appropriate reaction to the severity of the situation. Once we accept this, stop discounting it, and learn to respond appropriately, the wound starts to heal, and we find ourselves responding with a different reaction. After a while, we'll stop responding emotionally at all. That doesn't mean all our emotions are gone, but that we are in control of them, rather than they being in control of us.

Don't let people who can't handle their own emotions label you. How could a natural response be anything other than the right one? Whenever you respond to your instinct, you are being guided in a direction that is always right for you, that will lead you in the safest direction for you. Would a tiger stop and ponder basic instinct? I don't think so.

Led by Dorothy, the Lion, the Straw Man, and the Tin Man sought the power of Oz to give them courage, brains and a heart. The wizard was a sham—in that he had no magic power to create change from without. He was a true teacher, though, in his ability to bring forth change from within. The man who had masqueraded as the Great Oz said to the Cowardly Lion, "You have plenty of courage, I am sure. All you need is confidence in yourself. There is no living thing that is not afraid when it faces danger. True courage is in facing danger when you are afraid, and that kind of courage you have in plenty."

"If your core belief is that you're not doing it right, or you don't know how to do it right, you'll never get it. You're not perfect or you wouldn't have been born."

"Peace and healing in the world must begin within ourselves. As Ramana Maharshi, the Indian sage, once said: " As we are, as is the world." Ram Dass

The easiest thing in the world is to be ourselves, the hardest thing is to be what other people want us to be. Susan Ariel Rainbow Kennedy (Sark) is a free spirit who lives in a magic cottage in San Francisco. Her purpose in life is to be a beacon of light to the world. Sometimes she just takes naps with her cat Jupiter. Sark writes books between naps. I discovered her writings one day at the Henry Miller Museum in Big Sur, California, and its simplicity and joy helped change me. I sell her books for her and each is wonderful. Somewhere in the middle of *Inspiration Sandwich* Sark writes:

I AM ENOUGH
I DO ENOUGH
I HAVE ENOUGH

DANCING WITH TIGERS

Repeat those words several
times a day as you would a mantra.

*There is nothing I need do, need say, need perform, need
be, that I am not already. When I am sitting quietly,
enjoying peace, quietly answer the voice that comes up in
me telling me that I should be doing something. I will say
"Thank you for sharing," but "I am enough, I have enough,
I do enough." I am quite perfect the way I am.
If I were meant to do something else, it would be coming
up as a desire in me. But it isn't right now.
I am meant to sit, to rest, just as the trees
and flowers rest, as the birds and fish rest .
I have the right to be, without doing anything.*

*"Sitting quietly, doing nothing.
Spring comes and the grass grows by itself."*
Zenrin. *The Gospel according to Zen.*

When we judge, we hate. When Jesus taught his fol-
lowers not to judge themselves or others, he wasn't just saying they should be "nice." He was speaking to the subtle
violence we create in our own lives when we judge, and
was also referring to the deep healing that arises when we
walk in healing and peace with ourselves. Let's let ourselves
be. Whatever comes up for us is right.

*"The weapon with which we would destroy the enemy
must pass through our own heart to reach them."*
Thomas Merton.

DANCING WITH TIGERS

We try so hard to be what we're not, to get approval, to be liked, to be exceptional so everyone around will notice our wonderfulnes and in turn, love us. But Joseph Campbell describes the ability to be humble and ordinary as a doorway to love and understanding:

"The umbilical point, the humanity, the thing that makes you human and not supernatural and immortal— that's what's lovable."

If I'm dependent on you as a source of self-esteem, I demand that you be as I need you to be. Anything else or any less threatens my source. I need to control how you think, how you act, what you are, what you look like so that you'll be what I perceive that I need to meet my needs; you need to be my "ideal projected self."

How quickly do we pass judgment on others? Do we often find something wrong, something that could be improved? Do we pass a critical eye over everything that we see, and often can't wait to make suggestions for improvement? As we become healthier, we find that our judgments reduce. We judge others to the degree that we judge ourselves.

DANCING WITH TIGERS

As we cut down our self-judgments, we notice a feeling of peace in our relationships with others because we judge others less. When we accept ourselves as imperfect but OK beings, we'll inevitably accept others.

That doesn't mean that we'll always be pleased with the people in our lives, or invulnerable to hurt or rejection. But we're better able to accept other people for who they are, rather than trying to make them fit our image of who we want and need them to be. Because we're more satisfied with ourselves, we feel less pressure to fulfill our needs through others; consequently, we're better able to be a loving partner, parent, or friend.

"Love it the way it is."
Thaddeus Golas in *Lazy Man's Guide to Enlightenment*

LETTING GO

The physical Law of Clearing is that nature abhors a vacuum. Any property when removed, will always be replaced. When you make room in your life, something else will fill it up.

Last year two mountain climbers were making a difficult ascent. One of the pair broke his leg and kept climbing, pain and all. It was toward sundown when the lead climber passed a crevice, reached over to the other side, and just managed to grab on to a hold. The second climber lost his footing and began to swing wildly on the rope attached to the climber higher up. There they were—the higher climber hanging on to both sides of the crevice, the second climber with the broken leg helplessly dangling below, 2000 feet above the canyon floor. The first climber had three options: He could try to let go and shift his weight to pull them both over to safety; stay there until he weakened and lost his grasp; or he had to free himself of his friend and let him drop to the canyon floor below.

After three hours of agony, he made the decision to cut the rope. He managed to swing himself up to a ledge, and climbed back to base camp the next morning. Two days later as they were packing up to leave, one of the other climbers noticed a moving form on the distance, small at first but growing larger. It soon became apparent that it was the climber who was presumed dead. As it happened, when the rope was cut, the second climber was freed to fall. What the first climber didn't know, because he out of earshot from the second climber, was that there was a ledge about six feet below the injured climber, and cutting the rope allowed him to fall onto it and scramble to safety. If the rope hadn't been cut they both would have died.

What do you need to give up or cut loose that might be dragging you down? Maybe a rule, a person, a place? If you're keeping this through guilt or fear, cut the rope or you'll live a half life for the rest of time. Anyone who does not support your spirit is not worth your time.

If we have done everything we can, and our needs are not being met, staying in the relationship may be too painful or restrictive to our growth. Often, we have to be the one to decide to cut the rope and leave.

When we change, the changes we undergo can be intolerable to the people in our lives. Our partner or friend may take the initiative in ending our relationship. He/she may be used to things being "the way they've always been;" this can be the case even if things have always been bad. In "co-dependent" relationships, where boundaries cross like two concentric circles, one partner's frailty is the other partner's livelihood. The alcoholic who stops drinking, the overweight partner who loses weight, the perennial "loser" who begins to find purpose and discipline, all can be threatening to the balance of an unbalanced relationship. We might find that the "reward" for all our effort to grow and change is that our loved ones fight us at every step of the way, or even leave us. If this happens, we need to get people around us who support our growth, cut the rope on the others, and free them up to live at the level they wish.

Let's take time to honour what we've completed in the past and those steps we will take this year. Spend a moment and fill in the blanks. The following exercise helps focus on what's important and what needs to be given up.

The qualities I have best expressed in the past:

I acknowledge myself the most for:

The projects I have most recently completed:

The projects that I intend to achieve/complete are:

The goals/projects I have left incomplete and that I have no intention of completing and I hereby release are:

What I forgive and release about myself is:

My highest aspiration for myself is:

What I envision for myself in the future is:

The qualities I choose to experience and express are:

Since my life is my message, the message I wish to give is:

DANCING WITH TIGERS

There is a certain type of monkey trap used in Asia. First,
a coconut is hollowed out and attached by a rope to a tree.
Then, a small hole is made at the bottom of the coconut and
some sweet food is placed inside. The hole in the bottom is
just big enough for the monkey to slide her open hand into
the coconut, but not big enough for a closed fist to pass
through. The monkey smells the sweets, reaches in with her
hand to grab it, and then, with food clenched tightly in her
fist, she is unable to withdraw it. The clenched fist cannot
pass through the opening. When the hunters come, the
monkey becomes frantic, but it cannot get away.
There is nothing keeping monkey captive except the force
of her own attachment. All she has to do is open her hand,
let go, and she is free. Even so, it is a rare monkey that
manages to get away.

Old Legend

For the first solo flight in acquiring a private pilot
license, the FAA requires three take offs and three landings.
By my third landing, adrenaline caused "brain freeze," caus-
ing a few "bounce-and-go" landings. I soon realized I wasn't
going to land the plane. Then I remembered my instructor's
words: "Janet, takeoffs are optional, but landings are manda-
tory." So I had to figure out where I could crash so he
wouldn't see. Then I remembered what a jet fighter pilot
said when he was losing altitude fast: "O.K., Lord, let's
make a deal— you bring this plane down for me, I'll taxi it
in for you."

DANCING WITH TIGERS

Before I could rely on and trust myself and the knowledge I already had, I needed to give up control to the universe—to let it go—knowing that the laws that kept the plane in the air were the same that would bring it down safely. If I followed these rules, guidelines, and procedures, despite the fear I felt, I would land safely. It's so hard to communicate this trust that we all must have in the universe. A trust that the universe will always supply our needs if we trust it to. That as soon as we develop the courage to take a chance, there's always support under our footsteps.

One of my fears was not having enough money, traced back to my parent's issues and fears around money. The fear of not being able to provide for my children, of somehow failing, limited and confined me. Not feeling safe around money, I would work to lose whatever money I earned, through poor choices, inattention, wastage, but very rarely anything that gave me much pleasure. More often than I care to admit, I would leave my wallet out in open places, and then sense relief when it was stolen.

Two factors helped me with this: the first, recognizing my self-worth and that money was just one form of evidence of self-worth. Money was not evil; biblical references to money were misinterpreted and that it was a holy and Christian thing to accept money as a form of validation from the world. The only unhealthy aspect would be blockage of that exchange through hoarding or failing to accept what the world wanted to give me.

DANCING WITH TIGERS

The second factor was the period of time that while changing careers from a university faculty and private practice to speaking and writing, I had no money. I paid my mortgage with credit cards until my home was sold. I often wondered how I'd look pushing a blue plastic shopping cart. One day it hit me. "Right now, at this moment, I have everything I need. My children are healthy, the flowers in my vase are beautiful, the music on my stereo is beautiful, the candles are glowing. I'm safe and I have everything that I need."

Recognizing that although I had no money I was still safe, I could abandon the fear. I checked out the Joan Kroc Centre for the Homeless and found that it wouldn't be such a bad place. I traveled the shops on roller blades, except when the distances were too great, then I would ride my bicycle. I went to discount afternoon matinee movies, free noontime concerts, art shows, and gallery openings offering free food. During this six month period, I lived joyously, and without money.

Around this time, my three-year-old grandson Christopher developed into a great leader and teacher. One of the greatest gifts I was given was the gift of wandering around with him. We started where we were, had no destination, and Christopher, following his feelings, led me to places where he thought we should be. We wandered through city streets, stopping at whatever seemed to call us. One Saturday morning, Christopher needed to spend nearly three hours on the San Diego Trolley. *Three* hours.

DANCING WITH TIGERS

Christopher was my therapist in a session of flooding, or "prolonged exposure to a feared stimulus until the stimulus or event, person or situation no longer causes anxiety." My greatest fear was of wasting my life, of not being productive, fearing that if I wasn't productive I would be a less than useful human. In allowing those three hours to be lovng and accepting and fun, Christopher took me on another path. Let happen what will happen.

Start where you are and walk. Your starting point will be the situation you are in right now. Don't wait for other situations to emerge. They will never be the right one to start, because now is the right one. When you are finished using this one, the next one will appear. Then, use that one too.

If you have to know where you are going to walk, you only can go where you have already been. Just start out and the best way will be revealed to you. Gifford Pinchot, the author of Intrepreneuring, says "If you are 100% certain of the outcome of an action, what do you learn from taking that action? Not a thing. If you do not expose yourself to risk, you cannot possibly learn anything; if you risk nothing you learn nothing."

If you are sure of the destination, you will only go where you have already been. If you don't have a young child to follow around, borrow or rent one for a day, and do nothing but wander where he or she wants to go.

DANCING WITH TIGERS

*"The thing is to become a master and in your old age
to acquire the courage to do what children did
when they knew nothing."*

Henry Miller

*"Grown men may learn from very little children, for the
hearts of little children are pure, and, therefore, the
Great Spirit may show to them many things
which older people miss."*

Black Elk *The Sacred Pipe*

How many other old rules do we follow, unconsciously?

Can you complete these sentences?
If you can't say anything nice . . .
Clean your plate, there are . . .
Wear clean . . . Why? Because you might be in . . .
Don't speak until . . .
Sit up and keep your . . .

Which of these rules serve us, and which don't? I
wonder if it's time to scan our operating manual and strike
out those rules that no longer serve us. Rules that we
learned were taught by our early systems, in order to help us
adjust to our society at that time, whether that be our family, our school, our church, our community. It won't shock
you that one or more of these systems were probably dysfunctional, and taught us rules so that we could conform to
their dysfunctional system. They did so with the highest
intentions, through caring of the highest kind they could

give. But if the rules no longer serve us, carrying them is like applying slow pressure on the brakes of our car while trying to get up to top speed by flooring the gas pedal.

The rule "I'm no good, nothing I do is good, I'll never to amount to any good at all" is one of the most prevalent forms of self-victimization. The actor Anthony Hopkins lived in enormous self-doubt most of his life, covered with layers of alcoholism. Recently his simple, brief but completely real comments jumped at me from a page of a newspaper: "And that's what it's been ever since, letting self-doubts go. Because keeping them is not a form of humility but ego, getting the boot in before anyone else can. In 1975 I had to come to terms with crippling self-doubts, running away from responsibility, trashing things. The idea of 'I'm no good' is, finally, boring. And people take you up on it." The self-doubts Hopkins had now serve as the source of his greatest strengths. Without this soul-preparation, we wouldn't have Hopkins in "Remains of the Day," "Shadowlands," or "Silence of the Lambs." Use your symptoms, when they no longer serve you, let them go.

Use the terms healthy or honest instead of right and wrong or good and bad. There is no right and wrong, or good and bad, only sets of rules made up by people. The rules of the church were made by people. The rules of the educational system were made by people. Our parents made their own rules based on the rules of their dysfunctional families. These rules may not be healthy or honest.

DANCING WITH TIGERS

There is no right or wrong. One way of judging ourselves to be wrong is through self-doubts. Some of us think that self-doubts are a form of humility, or something charming, perhaps attractive to others, certainly spiritual. We can give them up more easily when we learn that pleasing a playful and joyful God is to live a life of joy, of fullness, and richness. Suffering comes naturally at certain junctures of life, we don't need to *create* it by self-doubt. Deliberate suffering and sacrificing lead us only into places of pain.

Let's not come from a place of suffering or self-doubt. Let's choose a place of power. We can make that choice. We're all grown up now, we don't need to ask permission to do what we need to do. We need to do what it is that we need to do, not to ask others if they think that its OK that we do it. If it needs to be done, there is, finally, no choice but to do it. Apologize afterwards if you need to, but never fail to do it because you asked for permission and weren't granted it.

We don't have to *fix* whatever no longer serves us, it's perfectly OK to just *let go* of it. It's not easy. We might need to let go of everything we thought our life was. That's fine, it doesn't mean we are letting go of our *life*, just our narrow definition of it. Whenever we replace an old definition for a new one, the new one is always bigger. Let's go for the biggest definition of our life that we can imagine. Jesus didn't say "Bring me your life, I'll fix it for you." He allows us to *let our lives go,* trusting that something new and better will come. It will.

MENTAL VIRUSES

There are two forms of thought that can develop into what I call "brain viruses," that is, they can spread wildly throughout our belief systems so that not one part of our conscious thought can evade them. They're responsible for much of the lack of happiness in the world.

Change and growth result not from adding anything new to what we are, but from treating and removing the viruses that invade us and sap our strength. Because there is no real cure for these, their treatment must be what we call "palliative" that is, we can treat the symptoms of the virus only. The virus remains dormant and can return at anytime. However, the symptoms controlled, we can live a perfectly fulfilled life. As our psyche develops resistance to the viruses, we become stronger.

Strength develops in resistance. We still wish a life of ease, with nothing to resist against? We wish not to combat these viruses? That's OK too, it's not time yet. Until we make the decision, though, there will be no outward manifestation of strength.

The first virus is: **"The Grass is Always Greener"** which causes us to want what we don't have.

This doesn't mean that we shouldn't change toward a better direction. It does mean to focus on what we have already gained, what we already have, and what we already know. What we pay attention to gets stronger, in ourselves or in other people. If we focus on what we don't have, that part of our thoughts strengthen, much like throwing fertilizer on only selected parts of our lawn. Don't throw fertilizer on what we don't want to grow. When we always want to be where we are not we can never be where we are. When we want what we don't have we can't appreciate what we do have. Appreciating and giving gratitude for what we have increases. Resenting what we don't have decreases.

The second is:**"Comparativitis"** or Comparing Ourselves to Others,

With this never-win virus, we measure ourselves with a yardstick that was custom made for someone else. There'll always be people more or less than we are at everything. If our early family honored certain characteristics, which we might or might not have possessed, this was our early yardstick with which we measured both ourselves and others. Whether it be intelligence, productivity, education, appearance, ethnicity, or whatever, we'll find that our judgments in these areas will be merciless until we examine our early yardsticks and give ourselves permission to let them go.

How could a violin compare itself to a piano? Or a Citabria acrobatic plane to a Citation jet? They all have different purposes. Measure your growth with your own yardstick.

DANCING WITH TIGERS

Water is for fish
And air for men.
Natures differ, and needs with them.

Hence the wise men of old
Did not lay down
One measure for all.

Thomas Merton in *The Way of Chuang Tzu Happiness*

KNOWING

Many of our world problems are caused by people who think they know what should be done, and then they try to force this knowledge on others. When we think of the most annoying people in our lives, they are those who are sure they have the answer for us, and can rarely hold back from their attempts to convert us.

We don't need to know. The more certain we are about something, the less we really know about it. Wisdom consists of the knowledge of not knowing. According to Carlos Castenedas, the third knowledge trap is clarity. When we're absolutely clear on something, that's the next belief system we have to give up to continue on our path of enlightenment. The clearer this knowledge is, the more attached we are to the belief trap.

"The intelligent man who is proud of his intelligence is like
the condemned man who is proud of his large cell."

Simone Weil in *A Life*

DANCING WITH TIGERS

The twin lions that guard the gates of Eastern temples represent confusion and paradox. If we want true wisdom have to pass through both. We don't know, and that's OK. Not having a clue is a very high state of being.

Ask: how can I find out? What can I trust as my source? All that I know is my own experience, so this is all I can trust. If I can't trust my experience, it means that I can only trust one part of my experience which tells me that I can't trust another part. There is no way out of this bind. I learn to always trust my experience which speaks to me in intuition, and I can trust my experience as long as I acknowledge that I may be wrong and probably will be at some later stage. And that is perfectly fine too.

"Is it not possible that middle age can be looked upon as a period of second flowering, second growth, even second adolescence? Signs similar to those in adolescence ... discontent, restlessness, doubt, despair, longing, are interpreted falsely as signs of decay. In youth one accepts these signs as growing pains, one takes them seriously, listens to them, follows where they head."
Anne Lindbergh in *Gift from the Sea*

It's often only as adults that we wonder if, contrary to evidence, we are not defects, and that we had the same mental apparatus as others, that our symptoms were only a warning sign of danger in the environment. That our anxiety around certain people served to warn us to get away. Typically, when we would feel these warning signs, they would lead us to explore further, to overcome that which was so uncomfortable within us. Our symptoms are a well-tuned warning system, that if heeded, will always steer us unswervingly in the right direction.

When we're anxious or frustrated, there is nothing wrong with us; a boundary has been threatened. Our boundary is our sense of identity that encircles us. We probably let other people in way too far and for too long, because we never learned about appropriate boundaries in our families. When we recognize that these symptoms are natural warning signs, we can begin to protect our boundaries whenever they are threatened, by telling others the effect they're having on us and requesting a change.

Perhaps we might not reach out far enough to get our needs met, or sometimes go way too far. As long as we're aware of this when it happens, and don't punish ourselves for it, it will self-correct when we get better at establishing and keeping our boundaries. We will always have a signal when our boundaries have been violated, and we must protect it.

When you're frustrated, ask yourself "which of my needs is not being met? How can I ask for it more clearly?" When you're anxious, you'll ask yourself "Who is threatening you or who has been inappropriate with you? Develop an automatic reaction to situations that bother you: "What do you feel, and what do you want?"

DANCING WITH TIGERS

This exercise may be helpful in learning to let go:

In your mind, form two screens divided in half. On the left side of the screen, picture something you need to give up. Someone you need to cut loose. If you can't see anything, that's fine. Allow yourself to sit quietly without knowing.

If you can imagine something you need to give up, on the right side of the screen, see what you have when that is gone. Focus on everything that's left. Feel its value. and recognize that you are enough, have enough, you do enough. Relax, breathe, you're safe. Your real potential may be buried under years of debris, and maybe you can't see it, but it's there. Believe that despite the lack of evidence.

If God believed she could make a more perfect choice than making you, she would have done it. The world owes you nothing but the universe owes you everything. You are good, you do care, you work hard, you give, you love. Honor that deeply. Cherish it. It's of deep value.

Keep your mind on the right screen: Think of someone in your life who was a warm supportive teacher, or guide. Someone who loved and accepted you unconditionally? If you can see this, feel that person for a moment. Then accept right now that the greatest gift you can give back to that person is to treat yourself the way this loving teacher treated you. Love means to look for the good.

TAKING ACTION

If we're always wishing that we had another hand of cards to play, we never get around to playing with the ones we've been dealt. One of my client's fondest dreams was to return to school and complete a university degree, a process she stopped when her children were born several years before. With some work, she recognized the false beliefs that had stopped her from returning to school for many years. As long as she put off returning, she could say to herself, "I could really be brilliant if I had an education. There would be nothing I could not do. I would win Nobel Prizes, Pulitzers, you name it."

In not trying, she never had to face the possibility, which she now has to face after completing her degree, that she isn't and probably never will be a Nobel Prize winner. And in overcoming the humiliating notion that she will never win a Nobel Prize, she can get on with accomplishing what she needs to do. Before that she was stuck in wishful thinking.

The wishful thinking once served her well. She wished to satisfy her mother's "insatiable" desires, "insatiable" because she could never make up for her mother's sense of inadequacy in who she was. Not wishing the ultimate disapproval, which she had anyway, she couldn't break out and make an attempt, giving herself the chance of freeing herself from her mother's expectations.

66

DANCING WITH TIGERS

A university professor, a colleague of mine, stored up his notes for over 30 years, planning to write a book. He had meticulously saved clippings and articles and notes in hundreds of folders that took up shelf after shelf in his office. I walked by his office on the day he was retiring and asked him what his plans were after retirement. He said, "I have got this book all set to go; I have been meaning to get it out for years. Now I'll finally have some time." Do you think he will really write his book?

How often have we had a really good idea and found that other people have stolen it later? The difference between our idea and the idea that made it to market is only one thing: action. It wasn't our intelligence or our appearance, our background, or the size of our clothing. It was only action. Somebody else took the idea and made it happen by acting, and moving forward for a long enough period of time until it worked.

Before taking action, if we have intention, wish, or thought, our action is already half complete. When we take action on your thought, it serves to complete it, or to gvie it form. Quantum Mechanics predicts that it is already done, we just need to "polish it off." When the Italian film director Frederico Fellini was asked where he got his ideas for films, he replied "The film already exists, it's a matter of looking around and finding it." Your thoughts crystallize the already existing matter in the universe, and your actions only polish it off. Whatever you dream or wish to do, consider it already done. Just take action, any action, just keep moving in the direction of your dream.

Until one is committed, there is hesitancy,
      the chance to draw back, always ineffectiveness.
Concerning all acts of initiative and creation,
      there is one elementary truth,
      the ignorance of which kills
      countless ideas and splendid plans.
That the moment one definitely commits oneself,
      then Providence moves too.
All sorts of things occur to help one that would never
      otherwise have occurred.
A whole stream of events issues from the decision,
      raising in one's favor
All manner of unforeseen
      incidents and meetings and materials assistance,
      which no man could have dreamed would
      have come his way.
Whatever you can do, or dream you can, begin it.
Boldness has Genius, Power, and Magic in It.
Begin it now.   Goethe

Don't travel down the highway of life looking through your rear-view mirrors at your "I wish I hads". Think of the grieving parents who lost their teenage daughter in a car accident. They buried her in her favorite mini-skirted red dress; one that they never let her wear because they did not want others to think badly of them.

One man, on the urging of his therapist, wrote a forgiving letter to his mother to whom he had not spoken in 20 years. Instead of mailing it right away, in his ambivalence he kept it for a few weeks, changing small parts of it here and there, making sure it was right. Three weeks went by, and one morning he received a phone call that his mother had died in her sleep the night before. When you have the urge to do something, it is meant to be done right away. When something lands on your path, pick it up.

A mother pinned a note to a photo of a young private on the Vietnam Memorial in Washington:

"I see you now on a black wall, a name that I gave you as I held you so close after you were born. As I held you, my hopes and dreams were of a good life for you, never dreaming of the few years we were to share. All that we loved ones can do now, is to come here and remember. I remember you as a baby, I remember your first day of school, I remember the love we shared and I remember the day you died. . . I miss you so much and the hurt never ends. You are still with us in your hearts and if anyone reads this, I hope they will remember that each name they see here was some mommy's little boy. So you are mine. Love Mom."

Five years from now as you reach out from the other side and greet yourself coming through the door, will you be proud of what you have done? Will you be able to shake your hand, pat yourself on the back and tell yourself that you did your very best? Will you regret the missed opportunities, the things you didn't do, the people to whom you didn't reach out in love. To dance with tigers, take action. Do it now.

CHANGING

We're programmed by nature to change, to take action, and if we're not doing it at a time when nature thinks we should, for own physical or emotional health, then we experience things as being "out of synch." The subsequent feelings of unrest, uneasiness,and dissatisfaction make this very clear. It's rather like one of those dual alarms on my clock radio, the first set to music and the second to a buzzer warning. I find it less painful to wake up to the music.

Nature has programmed a system whereby the awareness of the need for change happens only when we have the strength to make the change. So it is impossible to sense the need for change and be incapable of making it. If you weren't capable of the change, you wouldn't be aware of the need to make it. That's what insight and denial are about.

If we choose not to make changes, the clash, mismatch or out of synch feeling will be unbearable to our emotional and physical systems, and it will try to cover it up with whatever addiction is currently available to us, whether it be work, pre-occupation, smoking, overeating, alcohol abuse and so on.

Each cycle of change takes us to a deeper level. Lessons are repeated until they're learned, but although it comes up again, don't conclude that you messed up the first time. Change happens in a spiral upward, two twists up and one twist back. Sometimes three twists back. That's OK. The lessons get deeper and deeper according to the height of the spiral. The spiral of growth knows just where it should be and the lessons given you on the path are the perfect ones for you at that stage of your journey.

To everything there is a season and a time
        to every purpose
        under the heaven:
A time to be born, and a time to die;
a time to plant and a time to pluck up that which is planted.
A time to kill, and a time to heal;
a time to break down, and a time to build up;
A time to weep, and a time to laugh;
a time to mourn, and a time to dance.
A time to cast away stones, and
        a time to gather stones together;
        a time to embrace,
        and a time to refrain from embracing;

A time to get, and a time to lose;
a time to keep and a time to cast away;

A time to read, and a time to sew;
a time to keep silence and a time to speak;

A time to love, and a time to hate;
a time of war, and a time of peace.

                              Ecclesiastes 3:1-8.

DANCING WITH TIGERS

Many of us during the change process, experience wild swings of mood. In the past, instability was thought to be a symptom of a clinical disorder. Not necessarily. Whatever you are changing will be out of balance. Conversely, anything confused and out of balance in your life is in the process of change. The natural process is to feel great for a couple of days and rock-bottom crummy for another couple. When things stabilize at your higher level of growth, these swings will even out. Above all, don't punish yourself for the swings and interpret them as a sign of mental disorder.

Let happen whatever wants to happen. On the days that you feel great, do your work, get your stuff done. On the days you feel rotten, just let yourself heal. Don't try to push through it. Let it be.

Every time we undertake and complete something that was hard for us, our self-esteem grows. But strength doesn't grow on completion, it grows in the spaces between the actions we take to finish something. The steps are only external manifestations of the growing strength. The real rewards lie in what happens in between. Completing gives a sense of pride, but it's in the striving that self-esteem grows the most. The more we actively engage in challenge, the more we realize that we have the potential to emerge as a stronger person.

As we strive, we begin to see ourselves as resourceful, capable, and resilient. We'll find ourselves redefining our relationships, behaving more assertively, becoming less willing to tolerate people who are energy drainers. Because our self-esteem doesn't depend on other people's approval, we're more free to choose people to be around us with whom we can be completely ourselves.

RESISTANCE

The old Oriental saying: "If a medium in which you wish to create offers no resistance, there can be no durable impression" means that unless you are resisted, you are not making an impact. If you put your finger in a bowl of water, then in ball of clay—only one medium gives you permanent change—the one that offers resistance. Resistance is healthy. Kids resist parents, students resist teachers, employees resist employers, prospects resist salespeople, marriage partners resist each other. Resistance encourages thought, solutions and action. Your attitude toward resistance will determine how successful you are in dealing with it. Let people resist you. Be patient. Change doesn't happen when we want it but happens for it's own reason.

If people resist us, they are getting stronger and we're making an impact.

"Rarely is it advisable to meet prejudices and passions head on. Instead, it is best to appear to conform to them in order to gain time and combat them. One must know how To sail with a contrary wind and to tack until one meets a wind in the right direction."
Fortune de Felice 1778

"If you want to convert someone to your view, go over to where he is standing, take him by the hand mentally and guide him. Don't stand across the room and yell at him, don't call him a dummy, don't order him to come over where you are. You must start where he is, and move from that position." Thomas Aquinas

If the other person is going to change at all, it won't be through telling him how he should behave. Fault-finding, moralizing, being a "psycho-pest" or leaving little dust-balls of negative energy around the place increases resistance. As hard as this is to swallow, any change in our relationships can only be brought about by changing ourselves. Because at the very first attempt to change the other person, a resistance response is set in motion. The more we push, the stronger he'll resist, and the greater the tug-of-war.

You will not win.
You may as well give it up.

BLAME

Don't wait until you're recognized and appreciated.
You won't be.

So many of us have been carrying around the notion that people in our lives should know what we want and need. How often are we disappointed? It's perfectly okay to state our needs and wants no matter what they are. Once we voice them, we're free to observe others reactions to our requests. Just as we wouldn't expect anyone to blame us for having specific needs or wants, don't blame others who are unable or unwilling to meet our demands. Discovering which people support or block our wishes and dreams can bring about some deep realizations about the people in our lives. Have you asked? You'll never know unless you speak out.

DANCING WITH TIGERS

Instead of being clear, we sit around and complain and moan about how hard life is and blame everyone else as if we expected Prince Charming to rescue us. If we don't take action and instead expect others to do anything for us we set ourselves up to resent them when they don't. When we resent, we're sitting in a waiting room—waiting until others treat us better and give us what we want. The door to that waiting room doesn't open from the outside, we have to open it and reach out to get what we need.

"Ask, and it will be given to you; seek, and you will find; knock, and it will be opened to you. For everyone who asks receives, and whoever seeks finds, and to whomever knocks it will be opened. Who among you, if your child asks for bread, will give them a stone? Or if they ask for a fish, will give them a serpent? If you then . . . know how to give good gifts to your children, how much more will God give good things to those who ask?"

Don't suffer damage any longer than you need to. By risking leaving a relationship or a job, we're admitting, "I messed up there. I made a wrong choice. " We're blocked from getting on with new risks as long as we resist that we made a mistake and continue to blame other people and situations for our outcomes. It is as though nature needs situations to be complete before she allows us to leave them. Being complete includes admitting responsibility for the choices that we made and giving up resentment. Resentment, like any other emotion, ties us to people and events. If we chose no longer to be tied, accept that you were there because of choices you made, forgive yourself for them and move on.

DANCING WITH TIGERS

We're either in reaction to or at the effect of life. We become what we do, and are a result of all of the choices we make and the small habits we have. Taking responsibility means that for everything that appears in our life, we are responsible. We may not be aware how we created it, or what it needs to teach us, but that there is something within us that needs to take responsibility for it. It is there to show us a mental challenge or block. Until we begin to take full responsibility for our own experience of life we have no hope of changing it. Whatever you take responsibility for you can change. Blaming someone else for any aspect of our lives puts the responsibility outside our control and thus makes us powerless to change it. We are trapped and imprisoned in blame until we take responsibility for it, then we can solve the pattern and become free.

"I am responsible for this experience, I'm grateful that it showed up in my life to teach me what I need to learn."
We're responsible for what's in our life.
Be *at effect* or *at cause*.
If your core belief is that you're not doing it right, don't know how to do it right, you'll never get it. You're not perfect, or you wouldn't have been born.

Ette Hillesum, a survivor of the Nazi camps, writes of the healing surrender into grief and forgiveness (cited in Muller, 1992, p.13):

"And you must be able to bear your sorrow; even if it seems to crush you, you will be able to stand up again, for human beings are so strong, and your sorrow must become an integral part of yourself; you mustn't run away from it.

"Do not relieve your feelings through hatred, do not seek to be avenged on all Germans, for they, too, sorrow at this moment. Give your sorrow all the space and shelter in yourself that is its due, for if everyone bears grief honestly and courageously, the sorrow that now fills the world will abate.

"But if you do instead reserve most of the space inside you for hatred and thoughts of revenge—for which new sorrows will be born for others—then sorrow will never cease in this world. And if you have given sorrow the space it demands, then you may truly say: life is beautiful and so rich. So beautiful and so rich that it makes you want to believe in God."

FEAR

The feeling of fear may rise for a number of reasons-not only in response to a feared stimulus. Physiologically, the chemicals aroused can be labeled as fear when they may just be general arousal or general discomfort of the nervous system. It depends on what's going on in the environment and in your body.

Jack Kornfield says the presence of fear may be a sign of growth, a moment in which we are "about to open to something bigger than the world we usually experience."

Fear may arise when we encounter those things that would heal us. The bible teaches that when the shepherds met with something they had never seen before—even though it was a miraculous moment filled with light, announcing the birth of the Christ-child—they were still afraid. Fear doesn't always mean danger. In the shepherds case, they had inadvertently bumped into God.

When we grow up in fear, we develop strategies for shutting off, hiding, and running away. But as adults when we move closer to fear, explore it, play with it, even dance with it, we discover our deep capacity to survive. The more we use our fear as a strength, without numbing out, hiding out, or armoring ourselves, the more trust we develop in our own resources, our own creativity, resilience, and wisdom.

DANCING WITH TIGERS

There is a Zen story about a general who, during a war, led his troops through the country, running over everything in his path. The people of one town, having heard the tales of his cruelty, were terrified when they heard he was coming in their direction, and they all fled to the mountains. The general marched into the empty town and sent his troops to search for any who remained. The soldiers returned and reported that only one person remained, a Zen priest. The general strode over to the temple, walked in, pulled his sword, and said, "Don't you know who I am? I am the one who can run through you without batting an eye." The Zen master looked back and calmly answered, "And I, sir, am one who can be run through without batting an eye." Hearing this, the general bowed and left.

Real security comes from a feeling of dependence on yourself, not on someone or something else. We often risk giving up what we perceive to be our security without recognizing that security isn't an objective value. It isn't out there, so how can you give up something that doesn't exist?

What are fears that block us? In the Judeo-Christian tradition, men are expected to surpass the father—to do better, take up the family name and run with it—but women are not to surpass the mother. We show allegiance to our mothers by maintaining the status quo. As a result, growth and change can be serious risks for both men and women. For the male, expectations may lead to a risk of failure; for the female, expectations may lead to a fear of success.

DANCING WITH TIGERS

*When it's time to let go, value the old belief
and the old behaviors. They served you well
for many years; honour their passing.*

The villages of South American hut dwellers were being infested with insects. They had one of four choices: to flee the village and travel to another site and rebuild; to burn the village down, thereby destroying not only the insects but everything else around; to ignore the insects, do nothing and hope they go away; or lastly, to destroy just the pests but remain in the village.

We're constantly faced with these decisions, especially in relationships. Many of us will "burn" the relationship before considering alternate solutions to get rid of the pests. At the first sign of infestation, we may be tempted to flee. Or we may stay put and attempt to ignore the pests that plague our relationships. Consider the downside of each: It can get pretty tiring moving villages at each sign of infestation; burning everything around is rather inconvenient and wasteful; to remain in an infested environment is uncomfortable. The only choice that makes sense, and creates the least wear and tear on both physical and mental health, is to destroy the pests.

Growing up, not many of us were taught to solve problems directly. Instead we learned to run from or ignore what plagued us, perhaps through denial or compulsions. Confronting our pests not only means we need to take responsibility for our reality, it also means putting forth the effort to salvage our relationships. Understandably, this solution seems overwhelming, since we were not taught the skills required in creating and sustaining rewarding and nurturing relationships.

We are supposed to be frightened when jumping off into the unknown. If we didn't get frightened, our biological system wouldn't be working. All choices are risky, even the ones made with seemingly safe outcomes. The late novelist, John Gardner, said of the true writer that "he lays himself wide open, dancing on the high wire without a net," but each time we dance on that frightening high wire, we learn to balance a little bit better the next time.

Author Larry Wilson analogies life during changing times to a swinging trapeze. To move to the other side, we have let go of one trapeze bar and spend a split-second in mid-air before grabbing the other. With practice and good timing, the second bar will be there when we need it. On those occasions when it isn't, our trust brings the net below us to catch us when we fall.

Dr. Carl Hammerschlag, a psychiatrist and storyteller who has for years lived and worked among the Native Americans of the Southwest, relays the Northwest Coast Salish tribe Legend of fear. Fear is an enormous two-headed snake, over sixty feet long. At each end of the snake there is a head which swivels in every direction. If you move, the fear-snake will come after you, slowly moving one end and then the other until it has you trapped. The only possible escape once it traps you between its heads, is to stand perfectly still. In so doing, the fear-snake will see itself in the other head, become horrified, and will slither away.

Parachutists have told me that the intellectual commitment to jump decreases as the altitude of the airplane increases. But they say you have to decide to *act*, you don't *think*. Up there, while signing a release, re-writing your will, having a full range of pre-death experiences, fear grabs hold. As soon as you jump, however, you lose all fear, adrenaline pumps in, and you scream and laugh all the way to the ground. Afterward, you're grinning ear to ear and laughing hysterically, and guess what you want to do. Yep, all over again! Imagine how you would feel if you decided not to jump.

"You gain strength and courage and confidence from every experience. You must stop and look fear in the face. You must do the thing you cannot do." Eleanor Roosevelt

"Unless you try to do something beyond what you have already mastered, you will not grow." Robert Osborne

A lobster decides she needs a new shell after she senses the pressure of her body against her old shell—similar to the psychological discomfort we feel when we need to make changes. She has to get rid of what is confining her, so she sheds the shell, and her vulnerable body is exposed for several hours with no shell until a new one forms. A decision to not change would mean defiance of nature's laws. She might reason: "I've grown accustomed to my old shell, it might be a little tight here and there but I can adjust. There may be nicks and blemishes but it has served me well. What would happen if I had no shell? Certainly a shell that doesn't fit is better than no shell at all. What if I *never* get a new shell? And what if while I am without, I get a disease or some other terrible thing? I may as well keep the old shell, because even if I live in misery, at least the misery is certain."

Not taking risks when you need to will feel like being a four-pound lobster in a two-pound shell. You'll *feel* when change is necessary. Make the change, nature knows when you need to.

In ancient Greek, there are two words for time. *Chronos* describes chronological time, in minutes, hours and years. *Kairos,* translated by the Bible as "the fullness of time" describes the deeper readiness of things to be born, to blossom in their own time. To everything there is a season.

As we change, we feel a strange mixture of emotions. It takes work and sustained effort to complete the Hero's Journey, but once we're determined, the connection that we have with that goal is impenetrable. Don't expect that the first day you try out something new it's going to feel immediately comfortable, just as when we put on a new pair of hiking boots we don't immediately hike the Appalachian. It's no different for you than for anyone else. Everyone who takes risks feels the same awkwardness, discouragement and fear as we all do.

DANCING WITH TIGERS

*If we don't change our direction,
we're likely to end up where we're going.*

Old Chinese Proverb

*"To one who waits all things reveal themselves, so long
as you have the courage not to deny in the darkness
what you have seen in the light."*

Coventry Patmore

Am I a percentage ahead now in any area than I was last year? Last month? Oliver Wendell Holmes tells us that it is not the destination in life that is important—it is the direction in which we are traveling. Improvement works by small increases.

*"Show me the person who never makes a mistake,
and I will show you the person who
never makes anything."*
unknown

"Never, never, never, never give up."
Winston Churchill

*"Effort only fully releases its reward
after a person refuses to quit."*
Napoleon Hill

*"Few things are impossible to diligence.
Great works are performed not by strength, but persistence."*
Samuel Johnson

DANCING WITH TIGERS

*"It is not whether you get knocked down.
It is whether you get up again."*
Vince Lombardi

Let's think of each rejection as one step closer to achieving our goal. All we have to do to succeed is to increase our rejection rate. As Gene Olson in Sweet Agony said, "Failure exits only in pure form when you die not trying anything."

Failure seems to be a prerequisite for success—it frees us to take risks we might not otherwise take. After all, when you are at the bottom, there is no where to go but up. Failure really is positive.

There are no failures, only outcomes.

TOUGH TIMES

One of the toughest lessons we learn is that it's in the lowest times that we receive our highest good. On the opening page of Scott Peck's *The Road Less Traveled,* it states:

"Life is difficult. This is a great truth, one of the greatest truths. It is a great truth because once we truly see this truth, we transcend it. Once we truly know that life is difficult—once we truly understand and accept it—then life is no longer difficult. Because once it is accepted, the fact that life is difficult no longer matters. Most do not fully see this truth that life is difficult. Instead they moan more or less incessantly, noisily or subtly, about the enormity of their problems, their burdens, and their difficulties as if life were generally easy, as if life should be easy. They voice their belief, noisily or subtly, that their difficulties represent a unique kind of affliction that should not be and that has somehow been especially visited upon them, or else upon their families, their tribe, their class, their nation, their race or even their species, and not upon others. I know about this moaning because I have done my share. Life is a series of problems. Do we want to moan about them or solve them? Do we want to teach our children to solve them?" (p.15).

DANCING WITH TIGERS

A blind man was brought to Jesus and asked, "Rabbi, who sinned, this man or his parents, that he was born blind?" They all wanted to know why this curse had befallen this man. Jesus answered, "It was not that this man sinned, or his parents, but that the works of God might be made manifest in him." Instead of looking for the source or reason for suffering, look for the lessons that it can teach us.

The Buddha said that, during this life, we will experience "ten thousand joys and ten thousand sorrows." Suffering is woven through the fabric of all lives. All that we desire and what we own will pass away. We will someday lose everything. With these losses we experience suffering. This, said the Buddha, is the First Noble Truth. Jesus said: "In the world you shall have tribulation." The poor and wounded would "always be among us," and that even he could not escape from the pain of the world. This suffering is a part of the journey, and it is in its darkness that we learn the secrets of the spirit.

"When there is no longer a cyclone, there is no longer an eye. So the storms, crises and sufferings of life are a way of finding the eye. When everything is going our way we do not see the eye and feel no need to look for it. But when everything is going against us, then we find the eye."
Bernadette Roberts

"Troubles will come, they are always temporary—nothing lasts forever. Thus, there is the famous legend that King Solomon, the wisest man of all times, had a ring inscribed with the words, 'This too will pass.'"
Rabbi Aryeh Kaplan

DANCING WITH TIGERS

*And God said . . . I do set my bow in the cloud, and it shall
be for a token of a covenant between me and the earth. And
it shall come to pass, when I bring a cloud over the earth,
that the (rain)bow shall be seen in the cloud.*
                                                    The Book of Genesis

*See! I will not forget you . . .
I have carved you on the palm of my hand.*
                                                    Isaiah 49:15

Many of us were trained that in order to achieve
"goodness" or a final art form pleasing to God, that we
needed to sacrifice all, or part, of our lives. The higher the
sacrifice, the better. With that concept, our needs not being
met, we are driven by anger and resentment. Driven by
anger, we experience tremendous mood fluctuation from
being out of balance. It is not your job to sacrifice, you are
one of nature's playful creatures, you have a right to your
needs being met without giving anything up.

Resentment is damaging to the human spirit. Believe
you're worth letting it go, and that you don't need to punish
yourself any longer. We are where we are because of what
we believe we are. We are where we are because of the
choices we made. What we did was only what we could
do. If we could have done differently, we would have. We
always choose the highest possible course of action open to
us at any given time. Now, there is a higher course of action
open to you. Then there wasn't. That's perfectly all right.

DANCING WITH TIGERS

What if the purpose of our existence is to become truly loving, and through that love find our way back to the divine source. Think what if we find our freedom through struggling against darkness. Where would Luke Skywalker be without Darth Vader? How would Jacob have walked across the Jabbok River to claim his new life without first fighting the angel who crippled his thigh? Would Camelot have been so terrific if Arthur had been handed it on a silver platter? Dark nights can awaken First Stories of freedom, or they can reinforce the belief that we are powerless. The choice for bondage or freedom is ours.

"We teach our people that mistakes are like skinned knees for little children. They are painful, but they heal quickly and they are learning experiences. My people are covered with the scars of their mistakes. They have lived out in the field they are being shot at; they have been hit in every part of their bodies and they are real. By the time they get to the top, their noses are pretty well broken. The chances of their getting there with a clean nose are zero. They get there by producing and the by-product is to make mistakes."
Ross Perot

Maybe you remember the Japan Airlines plane that landed in the water just short of the runway in San Francisco airport a few years back. During the FAA and the NTSB investigations after the crash, Captain Asoh was called to the stand. After taking his oath, he was asked the reason, in his own words, of the cause of the disaster. He replied quietly and simply, "Asoh screwed up." His simple admission of making a mistake terminated a lengthy and costly investigation. It is all right to admit that you messed up.

DANCING WITH TIGERS

When we decide to change, we'll naturally try to revert back to the way we were. This isn't a sign of a weakened will. We might begin to change, then fall off, and if we take that as a sign of defeat, we might quit without realizing that we're meant to go back and forth.

A visitor to the cockpit of a 747 jetliner noticed an auto pilot warning buzzer and commented on it, "your airplane is off course, should you not do something about it?" The captain shrugged and said, "It's off-course 99% of the time. It constantly corrects itself." What is important is that we know our track or course well enough, that if we make course deviations we can climb back on track, not that we never get off course.

Lee Iacooca said, "You are never going to get what you want out of life without taking risks. Remember everything worthwhile carries the risk of failure." Henry Ford said, "Failure is only the opportunity to begin again." Even the average multi-millionaire has gone bankrupt 3.75 times. As Tom Peters said, "The essence of innovation is the pursuit of failure—to be able to try things and make mistakes—without getting shot."

We've failed many times, although we may not remember. We fell down the first time we tried to walk. We almost drowned the first time we tried to swim. We swung out the first time at bat. Let's not worry about failure. Let's worry about the chances we miss when we don't even try.

DANCING WITH TIGERS

Let's be ready to give up our ideals of the path as we travel it. There is no shame in admitting our mistakes. Mahatma Gandhi once led a protest march in which many thousands of people left their jobs and homes to endure great hardship. As the march was well underway, Gandhi called a halt and disbanded it. His lieutenants came to him and said, "Mahatma-ji, you can't do this; the march has been planned for a long time and there are so many people involved." Gandhi's answer was, "My commitment is to truth as I see it each day, not to consistency."

"The greatest regrets I heard were not from those who had taken a risk and lost. Invariably, they felt proud for having dared, and even educated in defeat. The real regret, bordering on mourning, came from those who had not taken chances they had wanted to take and now felt it was too late." Ralph Keyes

If I Had My Life To Live Over

"I'd dare to make more mistakes next time. I'd relax
I would limber up.
I would be sillier than I have been this trip.
I would take fewer things seriously.
I would take more chances. I would take more trips.
I would climb more mountains and swim more rivers.
I would eat more ice cream and less beans.

I would perhaps have more actual troubles but I'd have
fewer imaginary ones. You see, I'm one of those people who
live sensibly and sanely hour after hour, day after day. Oh,
I've had my moments and if I had it to do over again, I'd
have more of them. In fact, I'd try to have nothing else. Just
moments. One after another, instead of living so many years
ahead of each day.

I've been one of those people who never go anywhere
without a thermometer, a hot water bottle, a rain coat
and a parachute.
If I had it to do again, I would travel lighter next time.
If I had my life to live over, I would start barefoot
earlier in the spring and stay that way later in the fall.
I would go to more dances.
I would ride more merry-go-rounds.
I would pick more daisies.

Nadine Stair (age 85)
Louisville Kentucky

Reprinted from Ram Dass Journey of Awakening p. 5

GUILT

Guilt is a form of anxiety that often shows up after decisions are made, and usually means that we're breaking someone else's rules and following our own. That means that we're doing something healthy. Let's not let guilt make decisions for us.

Guilt is a feeling of having done something wrong (or not having done something we feel we should have done). We feel guilty when we believe that we've violated some law or failed to live up to a standard, whether internal or external. We feel guilty when we think we've displeased a person whose judgment counts in our eyes.

Guilt can be donated by others, as when a parent puts a "guilt trip" on a child ("you kids go ahead—I'll stay home and check for lumps"); or it can be self-imposed. We make ourselves feel guilty when we label or victimize ourselves with "should" statements. For example, we may label ourselves selfish for wanting to spend money on clothing. We may also feel guilty when we want something we feel we "shouldn't" want, such as going away with friends over a holiday instead of spending it with our family.

Guilt will go along with almost any change we make. No one can move forward without leaving something—or someone—behind. We can't grow without turning our back on what we've known and been. We know that if we leave others behind as we change, we'll disappoint and upset them; perhaps they'll even feel betrayed. Because we know this, we're bound to feel guilty. This is a universal experience shared by all people as they grow up.

When one member of a family or group begins changing and growing, he or she threatens to upset the balance that has enabled the system to survive. An automatic response on the part of others is to discourage that change, since it threatens the system.

Let's not forget, however, that destruction accompanies *every* act of creation. The colonies that became the United States of America had to break their ties with Great Britain in order to give birth to a new nation. A sculptor has to destroy a piece of marble to make a statue. In the same way, we need to destroy what we've been in order to become what we're capable of becoming. Only sociopaths are capable of living guilt-free. Guilt is a sign that we're healthy.

Don't do anything you don't want to do. This isn't irresponsible. Good results usually come from acts that are done with your whole heart and whole will.

DANCING WITH TIGERS

I keep this excerpt from a scuba diving bulletin. It concerns the guilt surrounding a failed attempt at reviving someone after a drowning. I still react to it.

"You may perform a miracle—revive someone-
bring someone back to life!
That would be marvelous, wonderful.
He may stay dead—you did the best you could.
You can not make a dead person deader—
he just stayed dead.
The fact that you responded at all means you were
courageous—congratulations. You can decide whether to
respond or not. You can decide whether to stop or not.
It is your decision—you just have to live with your decisions.
Remember that you will make the
correct decision at the time you make it.
Cut yourself some slack do not hindsight yourself and run a
guilt trip for a decision made under stress."

Although nobody assigned me this role, I bore the responsibility for my father's suicide. Because I was compared to him, I thought that if *anyone* could relate to him and help him, I should. After he shot himself, I tried to save him, and I couldn't. Finally he stopped breathing. I've never been able to forgive myself, and although I'm beginning to relieve myself of some of the responsibility, I still have flashes of sudden death of the people I love, such as my children and grandchildren. The small passage above, as simple as it is, helps me to let the guilt go. We always make the highest decisions, and perform at the highest levels we can, given what is available to us. Always.

DANCING WITH TIGERS

When we feel guilty, we're breaking someone else's rules and keeping our own. Guilt does not mean we are doing something wrong.

Guilt and anger often get mixed up. For example, we felt guilty when we were angry at our parents or teachers. Anger and guilt got mixed. Maybe our parents and other adults used guilt to express their anger and get their needs met; anger and guilt got mixed. If anger wasn't one of the allowed emotions in a family, it probably was expressed only through shame or guilt.

Supposing you feel guilty because you don't call your mother more often. Are you angry because she never calls you? Supposing I feel guilty because I'm depriving my daughter of her third pair of jeans this season. Am I feeling angry that she's demanding these? When we feel guilty, we must ask ourselves "Should I be angry here instead? At whom or at what?"

When we start to follow our commitment to our own health, we may constantly feel guilty, rotating through shame every few days, then weeks, then months. Just as feeling guilty means that we're doing something healthy, however, feeling shame means we are breaking very old patterns. Not feeling the shame, and acting it out in destructive patterns is what destroys. Shame doesn't.

MANIPULATION

One of the strangest traps in which we can be caught is the web of manipulation. Being not conscious of our own boundaries, needing to be accepted, or even failing to recognize our own manipulative tendencies, the webs weave in and out seamlessly around our lives, trapping us in a quagmire of confusion.

This is a simple note to families from an eating disorders unit. I keep it in my daily calendar as a reminder of the boundaries we need to set in love. Although there may be no-one in your life with exactly these challenges, so many of us can so easily buy into manipulation.

AN OPEN LETTER TO MY FAMILY

I am an over-eater; undereater; vomiter. I need your help.
Don't lecture, blame, or scold me. You wouldn't be angry
at me for having diabetes or TB.

Overeating/undereating/vomiting are diseases too.
Don't hide my food; It's just a waste because I can always
find ways of getting more. Don't let me provoke your
blaming. If you attack me verbally or physically you will
only confirm my bad opinion of myself.
I hate myself enough already.

Don't let your love and anxiety for me lead you into
doing what I ought to do to for myself. If you assume my
responsibilities you make my failure to assume them
permanent. My sense of guilt will be increased,
and you will feel resentful.

98

DANCING WITH TIGERS

Don't accept my promises. I'll promise anything to
get off the hook. But the nature of my illness prevents
me from keeping my promises,
even though I mean them at the time.

Don't believe everything I tell you; it may be a lie.
Denial of reality is a symptom of my illness. Moreover,
I'm likely to lose respect for those I can fool too easily.

Don't cover up for me or try in any way to spare
me the consequences of my eating/starving/purging.

Don't lie to me, pay my bills, or meet my obligations.
It may avert or reduce the very crisis that
would prompt me to seek help.

I can continue to deny that I have an eating problem
as long as you provide an automatic escape from the
consequences of my behavior.

I love you.

No matter what your manipulator says, recognize
that he or she is functioning at the highest level possible at
that moment and is trying to get his or her needs met. The
method by which they're trying is not appropriate, however,
and you will not respond to it.

Stop the manipulation by agreeing in principle with
the guilt-inducing statement.

If you value the relationship and want to improve
communication, you may want to get discussion going and
not just cut off the manipulation. If someone is using anger

with you, ask what it is about your behavior that's so upsetting. The question forces the other person to clarify the personal, subjective basis for the criticism. That makes open discussion possible. A healthy response is to stop what you're doing as a response to manipulation, but if you do, don't punish yourself, or fall into the victim role, which causes you to resent the people who "hold you back" or "make you do things." Manipulators go only for easy prey. You're manipulated only if you allow yourself to be.

All these can be manipulations:
- Being sick/developing physical symptoms
- Being extremely hard working or dedicated
- Getting angry at you
- Accusing you of .... (whatever you overvalue or disown).
- Becoming helpless and confused
- Blaming others
- Saying "I'm trying."
    "There is no try—there is only do or not do."Yoda
- Playing ignorant "I didn't know"
- Being silent or looking or acting hurt
- Crying, fainting, vomiting, bleeding
- Being very agreeable and cooperative
- Acting childlike, cute and innocent
- Flattery or attention
- Promising, but never delivering
- Withdrawing
- Forgetting or being late
- Being too busy, having had no time

Stay calm when blocking a manipulation • Don't reject the manipulator • Manipulation occurs only when it works • Not all manipulation is conscious • You can't prevent, avoid, or stop another's manipulation • Use your feelings as an antenna to judge whether or not you're being manipulated. If you feel you are, you are • When one manipulation doesn't work, there may be a backup strategy. Don't quit in your efforts. The manipulator is talented. Manipulations will continue until healthier methods are developed • Some manipulations represent serious emotional problems • When in doubt that you're being manipulated, buy time. You have permission to put off decisions • Manipulation gets worse before it gets better. If things deteriorate it's not a sign that you've failed, rather that the manipulator is bringing out bigger guns • Don't let it wear you down.

If the manipulator is part of your family, the pattern is caused by the system not the person using the strategy. Have love and caring as you stop it. Manipulations mean that this person's only method of being heard in this family is through this technique.

It's time to listen to what's going on.

EASE UP

Always interpret your behavior at the highest,
most compassionate level.

What absolutely locks us into old behaviors is the cycle of shame. This is how the shame cycle works:

We perform our old behavior, the one that served us well in the past but that no longer serves us, like overeating, procrastinating, getting involved with the wrong people, and so on. We find that we can't help it. We get into it, manage to stop it, and finally climb out. What stamps it in is the self-punishment that follows it, not the old behavior. The old behavior is just serving us when we need it, that's all.

Robin had various addictions throughout her life, none of which she was easily able to shake. She reasoned that if she punished herself for them, at least she would motivate herself to get over them. If she accepted them, it was like accepting defeat. And so the shame cycle stamped them all in. When she was able to recognize that each of them served her well given what she was processing or experiencing at the time, and she could become grateful that they showed up just at that time, she was able to use them as long as she needed to and, in good time, the need would drop off and the addiction would too. Punishment is a very powerful form of attention, and what you pay attention to gets repeated. Punishment serves to reinforce behavior.

DANCING WITH TIGERS

Shamu, the Orca whale at San Diego's Sea World, jumps in the air, soaks the first few rows of spectators, and everybody loves her. How come she can jump so high? Do you think the trainers went out into the ocean and said, "All you whales who can jump 50 feet, come to the boat!" No, they take an ordinary whale, put her in a pool, swim around with her to decrease her fear, and start the training. They put the rope under the water and every time she swims over it, she gets a pile of fish. Every time she swims under,she gets nothing. After a few times the whale starts to notice an interesting relationship, "Hey there is a no-lose deal here."

Slowly, she gets pretty consistent, and then they raise the rope, little by little rewarding every time she swims over, ignoring every time she swims under. Pretty soon the rope is out of the water, and getting raised higher and higher. The training never fails. Why do our risks fail?

We all want to jump 50 feet the first crack. If we don't have the patience to start with the rope under the water, we raise the rope too much too fast, before we're ready. We forget to reward ourselves when we go over, but remember to punish ourselves when we go under the rope. Do you think you will ever hear the trainers at Sea World yelling at Shamu when she goes under the rope, "You stupid whale! You blew it! I can't believe you went under that rope again. What a loser. You'll never jump 50 feet." I don't think so. If we want to perform consistently at high levels, we need to change our reward pattern or we'll never get out of the water.

DANCING WITH TIGERS

Self Talk is what we say to ourselves constantly throughout the day. We're not aware of how much we do self-instruct, but our subconscious mind is picking up on every comment—every silent command, and is working to follow orders.

"Do not focus on building up your weaknesses. Understand your strengths and place yourself in a position where these strengths count. Your strengths are what will carry you through to success." Peter Drucker

Write down what you've accomplished and done well on each separate line without prioritizing them. Stick it up in front of you. Keep it there. At night, run through what you did that day that made you proud or would have made you proud if you were a gentler master.

In our own mirror we can never see our talents, our gifts, qualities spirits, morals, what we stand for, believe in, live for are willing to die for. We see our zits, chin hairs and cottage cheese thighs because that's what this terrible oppression has done to us. Our physical obsession is a disease and it's our jug. It limits us by zapping our energy and time.

Love, in Greek, means to look for the good.

Let's listen for our hate messages and turn them off. Hate messages are strong because we work them. If our left arm were exercised with every self-destructive message, and our right arm not, our left arm would be strong and our right arm flaccid. What you pay attention to gets repeated. Whatever you do, gets stronger. When we begin to practice loving, nurturing thinking (the right arm), the attempts are flaccid, but if we continue them long enough, they become as strong and healthy as the left arm.

Although I'm not sure how this measurement was taken, according to Deepak Chopra in *Ageless Body, Timeless Mind,* the average human thinks 60,000 thoughts a day, 90% being the same thoughts as the day before. Our tormentor today is ourselves left over from yesterday. Protect your thinking: it's all you have that is yours. Others cannot invade it without your permission. They can take away your possessions, your loved ones, and your liberty but they can never take away your thinking. You choose that.

DANCING WITH TIGERS

1.   Stop all criticism. Criticism never changes a thing. refuse to criticize yourself. Accept yourself exactly as you are. You are just where you need to be for the lessons you need to learn. Everybody changes. when you criticize yourself, your changes are negative. When you approve of yourself, your changes are positive.

2.   Don't scare yourself. Stop terrorizing yourself with your thoughts. It's a dreadful way to live. Find a mental image that gives you pleasure and immediately switch your scary thoughts to a pleasure thought.

3.   Be Gentle and Kind and Patient. Be gentle with yourself. Be kind to yourself. Be patient with yourself as you learn the new ways of thinking. Treat yourself as you would someone you really loved.

4.   Be Kind to Your Mind. Self hatred is only hating your own thoughts. Don't hate yourself for having the thoughts. Gently change your thoughts.

5.   Praise Yourself. Criticism breaks down the inner spirit. Praise builds it up. Praise yourself as much as you can. Tell yourself how well you are doing with every little thing.

6.   Support yourself. Reach out to friends and let them help you. It is being strong to ask for help when you need it.

7.   Be loving to your negatives. Acknowledge that you created them to fulfill a need. Now you are finding new, positive ways to fulfill those needs. So lovingly release the old negative patterns.

Adapted from the poster
"How to Love Yourself" by Louise L. Hay.

DANCING WITH TIGERS

Treat yourself as you would a small child:

My hands are small,
I don't mean to spill my milk.
My legs are short.
Please slow down so I can keep up.
When I touch something bright and pretty,
Please don't slap my hands.
Please look at me when I talk to you.
I need to know you're listening.
Let me make mistakes without feeling stupid.
My feelings are tender.
Please don't expect the bed I make or
the picture I draw to be perfect.
Love me for trying.
Remember I am a child, not a little adult.
Sometimes I don't understand what you say.
Please love me for just being me.
Not just for the things I can do.
I love you. You're all I have.

THE TRUTH

Telling the truth is freeing; lying and covering up take a tremendous amount of effort. We lie to avoid discomfort, whether through anticipated rejection from others, when we think they'll find us inadequate if they know the real us, or to avoid the discomfort of confrontation.

If we don't tell the truth, which means not only saying things that we know in our heart and soul and not true, but also not saying those things which we know in our hearts are true, people will never know the real us. People sense when we're not being real, and will tend to avoid us not because of us but because they sense the danger of our anxiety. When we lie about ourselves, too, we stamp in the belief that we are so inadequate that we have to lie about ourselves.

The way we think influences the way we feel and behave. We can't change reality, but we can change the way we think about it. Events alone can't cause us to experience negative emotions such as fear, depression, and loneliness. However, positive statements that aren't true can't processed by our mind. Our mind will reject them like our body rejects foreign substances. Statements have to be realistic to be accepted. Statements that are realistic, not necessarily "positive," help.

Let's not look where we don't want to go or need to go. Let's not listen to people who discourage us. People will

108

criticize and discourage us when we're threatening to them. Ghandi said: "They cannot take away our self respect unless we let them."

"Just mere thoughts are as powerful as electric batteries as good for one as sunlight or as bad for one as poison.
To let a sad thought or a bad one get into your mind is as dangerous as letting a scarlet fever germ get into your body.
If you let it stay there after it has got in you you may never get over it as long as you live"
Frances Hodson Burnett

TRAVEL LIGHTLY

Travel together!

When we have a journey to travel together, let's do what the Canadian geese do. Geese fly in V-formation to create uplift for each other. They get 71% greater flying range. If we have common direction and sense of community we'll go faster. When a goose falls out, it immediately feels drag and resistance when alone. To take advantage of lifting power it falls back into formation. If we have any goose sense, we'll stay in formation and accept others help and help others. When the head goose is tired it rotates back and others take its place. It pays to take turns doing hard jobs. Geese honk from behind to encourage the ones in front because they have hard decisions to make. Make sure your honking is encouraging and not discouraging. When a goose is sick or wounded or shot down, two other geese follow it down and stay with it until it dies or flies again. If it flies again, they go together to look for another formation or they start their own.

And let's not get so serious that we forget to live life. When God created life she meant it to be fun. Kids play, dolphins jump. Our path is so serious anyway, don't make it worse than it is. Lighten up. This is going to be your whole life, so you may as well relax. Don't deny your passions. Sensory stimulation not acknowledged goes underground. We are a "re-creational" universe, let's re-create ourselves. Watch how kids play, dolphins jump, and birds sing. Mother Nature means us all to have fun.

INTUITION

Many of us learned to mistrust our own inuitive sense. If our families didn't talk about their feelings, we couldn't learn how to interpret the emotions we had, and ignorant of their origins, learned to mistrust them. If our parents were unable or unwilling to speak the truth, we began to mistrust our own perceptions of what was true. As we grew older, whenever we felt afraid, instead of protecting ourselves, we would focus our attention on our weakness. We would trust only one part of our experience, that part we interpreted as weak.

The strength we developed while growing up in our families can serve us well now, if we focus on what we've developed not what we lacked. We developed determination, spirit, and courage as we managed to maintain our lives, to survive repeated injuries, and to protect ourselves from danger.

Joan was the child of two alcoholic parents, who would in turn, come to each of the children after their drunken fights and demand promises of loyalty. Joan and her five brothers and sisters lived in a terror-filled, unpredictable world. For refuge, Joan often hid in the dark in the closet and it was only after a few months of therapy that she could admit one of her terrible secrets; that she still hid in the closet. After this admission, it took quite a bit more time before she could accept the strength of this action, and that she was perfectly free to hide any time she needed to, and

111

this action, even as an adult served, her well. It was only her shame of it that continued to damage her. We all have discovered a place of refuge deep within, where we found a source of strength. This safe place has been a trusted ally, and it's a place we can visit and use whenever we want, without shame.

Intuition will always guide us in the direction we need to go next. This "Voice of the Heart," is often drowned out by fear, which is the "Voice of the Head." When we are stopped through fear from speaking or acting, and we can't explain why, the reason happened many years ago—earlier than we can verbalize or explain. Question whether there's still a valid reason for not saying or doing what we want. When we are safe with this questioning, our Intuition can then again guide us. Our intuitive sense will never guide us to a place that is bad for us.

Women have a profound psychic intelligence. Because our power is feared, we've been thrown into pits, burned at stakes, put in steno pools. Unlike animal moms, our moms never taught us to avoid dangerous predators. So we submit and live in mental traps. How many of us have gone into bad relationships *knowing* better? *Stayed* in relationships past the time we *knew* we should leave? Everything we need is inside, would we only listen.

DANCING WITH TIGERS

On the day when it will be possible
For a woman to love not in her weakness
but in her strength
Not to escape herself but to find herself
Not to abase herself but to accept herself
On that day love will become for woman as for man,
A source of life and not a mortal danger.

Simone de Beauvoir

    Dr. Joan Borysenko, a psychologist and cell biologist, and author of *Fire in the Soul,* tells the story of a mother and daughter who were involved in a head-on collision. They both experienced near-death light and asked for a "higher truth," that is, asked to what greater good needed to be served by their next actions; whether death, returning to the world in a comatose state, or returning with minor injuries. The higher truth responded that no greater good would be served by any other than returning with minor injuries, which is what happened. When our actions are in alignment with the greater good or higher truth, they will always be supported by Spirit and no power in the universe can ever be against them. Spirit always supports its own expression.

    All our experiences in life are a way of nature demonstrating our next lesson to us, or manifesting itself in us. The neat things that happen to us are just a way nature has of showing up in our lives. They aren't necessarily caused by us, they are, however, our awareness of spirit in our lives. Each time we notice how much we have, focus on our Blessings, we simply are being aware of what is always available to us, at whatever level and extent we wish. Whatever we are grateful for will increase. As long as we are attending to these manifestations, and attention increases each phenomenon, then whatever we are attending to will increase. If the blessings of our life are in our attention, they will increase, not because they aren't already there but because our awareness enlarged our scope or vision to sweep more into our consciousness.

You are either manifesting your good
or your blockages to it.

ENOUGH

Reverend Kathy Hearn relates the story of Scare City, in which nobody has enough:

Scare City was a walled city near a wonderful ocean and beautiful surroundings. Inside Scare City, people were very busy, and there was a strange atmosphere. People were very busy, and they had the belief that there wasn't enough to go around. Parents had positive intentions but children grew up with not enough of anything, not enough time, money, attention, playing, hugs. Their belief was that "Care is in short supply-we can't waste it. "If I give, I won't have." "If I take, I am selfish." The Scare City contract was: "I will take care of you if you take care of me" and everybody traded little thimbles of caring. Everyone kept score. If someone gave, he waited to get something back. Care was in such short supply, that people latched onto whatever promised care whether the source was suitable or not, whether it caused harm, or if it were deadening to the spirit. The prevailing belief was: "Hold on! At least I have something. Better just settle for it. Something else might not come along."

It was hard to make decisions in Scare City, because you could make a mistake and end up with less, so everyone postponed decisions. With a reduced sense of possibility in their lives, their lives grew small and sparse. "Ask and ye shall be ignored." People just stopped asking because they thought "Why bother?" Because it had been so long since their needs were met, they began to lose sense of what they truly needed. Because of this, they became hurt, angry deprived, and cheated, and this filled their thoughts and dreams. Some people began to demand. You could hear them crying: "As a kid I gave away, but now I deserve. There was some energy and empowerment, but the foundation of thought never changed, so the old fear and guilt always came back. Others in the city set out to get as much as they could, so they could have more--and they suffered from unending desire. The more they got, the less they felt good about.

Then one day, two citizens of Scare City left the walls and traveled to a distant city called "Enough". When they entered the city boundaries, they began to hear strange words that they had never heard before such as: abundance, plenty, prosperity, and satisfaction. There was a state of mind called abundance. One could give love without fear of loss. Because there was enough for everyone and abundance of all things, it was OK to receive without guilt, because receiving didn't mean you were depriving anyone else.

Soon word began to spread back to Scare City, of this strange new land where everyone had enough. So few believed it, that not many ventured out. Some who did arrive in Enough left the city out of fear, because they could not trust this new place. Others stayed long enough to start to believe in enough too. Every step they took, whatever path they took, led to enough. With dreams of enough filling their minds and hearts, they started sharing. As they began to focus on what was given to them everyday, they too started to live in a land of plenty!
And nobody kept track.

"Abundance is not in things or what flows in, but rather what overflows from your heart." Abundance is a gift already made—just move into alignment with it and take away blocks to receiving it.

When the affairs of our life are in order, we'll always experience a sense of peacefulness and freedom. The key to developing order in anything is attention or concentration.

DANCING WITH TIGERS

Until we're ready to give anything our attention, it will always be in a state of disorder, or chaos. If our financial affairs are in chaos, for example, more money will not solve the problem, it will only bring more chaos. If our relationship patterns are in chaos, for example, more or different relationships will not solve the problem, it will only bring us more chaos.

The universe is always in the process of keeping itself in perfect balance. If we lie, the universe will balance this somehow. If we take more than we give, the universe will extract energy from us in another way. For example, if we spend more money than we have, the universe will keep things in balance by extracting from us, in whatever form it is available, usually our life energy. If we hoard, or keep more than we need, the universe will take from us in another way. Both behaviors are based on a belief that there is not enough to go around and so this will be confirmed.

It's not what you're doing in life,
it's who you are while you are doing it.

"Sometimes I have to erase my mind and just keep doing what I believe is true. If you are doing something you would do for nothing–then you are on your way top salvation. And if you could drop it in a minute and forget the outcome, you are even further along. And if while you are doing it you are transported into another existence, there is no need to worry about the future."

George Sheehan, PhD.

EPILOGUE

One day Tigress found herself far away from home. A cloud passed over the sun and this made her think, and think, and think. She sat under an olive tree and thought, "What will happen to me when the earth comes to an end?"

At that very moment the wind stirred up and several large ripe olives fell from the tree, landing on her nose. The Tigress ran off as fast as her strong legs could go. So sure was she, that the noise of the olives falling was that of the earth breaking to pieces. So she ran.

An eagle saw Tigress running and flew down to ask her what was wrong. "Run for your life!" yelled Tigress. "The earth is falling to pieces!" The eagle began flying away as fast as she could.

A bear saw Eagle and Tigress and called after them to find out what was wrong. When she heard that the earth was falling to pieces she began to run as fast as she could to get away.

A snake saw Bear, Tigress, and Eagle and called to them. "SSSSlow down. Where are you going ssssso fasssst?" By this time Bear, Tigress and Eagle were very tired, so they slowed down to tell the snake about the earth falling to pieces.

Snake smiled. "I don't sssssee the earth falling to pieccessss," the snake hissed. Bear and Eagle looked around them, and then at each other. Then the three of them, Bear, Eagle and Snake, looked at Tigress. Tigress became very uncomfortable.

DANCING WITH TIGERS

Tigress told Bear, Eagle and Snake she had indeed heard the earth falling to pieces. Why else would she have run away so fast? They determined that someone must go back to the place where Tigress had heard the earth falling to pieces to see if it was so.

Bear said, "I will go back. I'm the biggest and the strongest and I'm not afraid."

Eagle said, "I will go. I can see the lay of the land and get the big picture."

Snake said, "I will go. I have my head to the ground. I feel the vibration of what's going on."

But Tigress shook her head. "I must go back," she said. "For only I know the place to go, but I need you all to come with me. For I am afraid to go alone. If we all travel together, Bear, Eagle, and Snake, we have a better chance of arriving there safely and learning what we must know." And so they did.

As they journeyed to the spot where Tigress heard the earth falling to pieces, Eagle flew up high to get the larger picture. Bear lumbered along, sniffing the air, keeping alert to any danger. Snake slithered forward, always keeping her head close to the ground. And Tigress led the way. For she knew where they all had to go.

Finally, they arrived at the place where Tigress had heard the earth breaking into pieces. It was quiet and calm. Tigress approached the exact spot where she had heard the noise. There, on the ground, was a beautiful grouping of black olives Suddenly, another olive landed on Tigress, smearing another strip of black on her lovely coat. Bear, Snake, Eagle and Tigress surrounded the fruit.

"Is this what frightened you, Tigress?" they asked. Tigress was embarrassed. She stood there, silently. But then she looked up into the tree under which they stood. There she saw thousands of beautiful, ripe, delicious olives. And one by one, more and more juicy, ripe olives fell on Tigress, each one marking her shiny coat with a black stripe.

"Yes," she said. "My fears led us away from here, but look! Together we have found a wonderful, new place, rich with fruit. And from that day on, Tigress' coat was striped with black as a sign of her courage. "

All agreed that this was a wonderful place. They lived happily there together for many years, until the next time the earth fell to pieces.

Based on an old Indian legend

AFTERWORD

The great beast materializes out of the dusk like a dream -- a striped vision of might and mystery. Emerging from a thicket, the Bengal tigress is hungry and ready to begin another night's hunt. Fortunately, Nature has given her the prowess to prey upon creatures far larger than herself. Her massive shoulders and forelimbs can grip and bring down animals weighing more than a ton.

For millenniums, tigers have prowled the minds of humankind as surely as they have trod the steppes and forests of Asia. On the banks of the Amur River in Russia, archaeologists discovered 6,000-year-old depictions of tigers carved by the Goldis people, who revered the tiger as an ancestor and as god of the wild regions. In Hindu mythology the goddess Durga rides the tiger. And Chang Tao-ling, a patriarch of the Chinese philosophy of Taoism, also mounts a big cat in his quest to fight evil and seek the essence of life. In the English-speaking world nearly every schoolchild is familiar with William Blake's attempt to frame with words the tiger's "fearful symmetry." India's Valmik Thapar, a student of tiger lore, says British and Dutch colonists sometimes killed the beasts in Indonesia and China as a way of asserting their supremacy over local deities.

All too soon, though, dreams may be the only place where tigers roam freely. If Asian cultures no longer revere the tiger as a god, many still believe that the animal is the source of healing power. Shamans and practitioners of tradi-

121

tional medicine, especially the Chinese, value almost every part of the cat. They believe that tiger-bone potions cure rheumatism and enhance longevity. Whiskers are thought to contain potent poisons or provide strength; pills made from the eyes purportedly calm convulsions. Affluent Taiwanese with flagging libidos pay as much as $320 for a bowl of tiger-penis soup, thinking the soup will make them like tigers. A beautiful tiger skin may bring its seller as much as $15,000, but the bones and other body parts generate even more money, and they are much easier to smuggle and peddle. As incomes rise in Asia, people can afford to pay tens or hundreds of dollars for a dose of tiger-based medicine. And as the destruction of tigers decreases supply, the price of their parts rises further, creating ever greater incentives for poachers to kill the remaining animals.

Until now, the tiger has always been extraordinarily adaptable and resilient. But the tiger has finally run afoul of humanity, an evolutionary classmate that has proved to be an even more resourceful killer.

Saving the tigers means saving ourselves.
Dancing with tigers means loving ourselves.

REFERENCES

Borysenko, Joan (1993). *Fire in the Soul*. New York: Warner Books.

Campbell, Joseph A. (1988). *The Power of Myth*. New York, Doubleday.

Campbell, Joseph A. (1993). *The Hero With a Thousand Faces*. New York, Doubleday.

Canfield, Jack & Hansen, Mark V. (1993). *Chicken Soup for the Soul*. Deerfield Beach, FL, Health Communications, Inc.

Chopra, Deepak (1993). *Ageless Body, Timeless Mind*. New York: Harmony Books.

Csikszentmihalyi, Mihaly (1990). *Flow: The Psychology of Optimal Experience*. New York, Harper & Row.

Csikszentmihalyi, Mihaly (1993). *The Evolving Self*. New York, Harper Collins.

Dass, Ram (1990). *Journey of Awakening A Meditators Guidebook*. New York, Bantam Books.

Hammerschlag, Carl A. (1989). *The Dancing Healers*. New York, HarperCollins.

Hammerschlag, Carl A. (1993). *The Theft of the Spirit*. New York, Simon & Schuster.

Houston, Jean (1992). *The Hero and the Goddess*. New York, Ballantine Books.

Moses, Jeffrey (1989). *Oneness: Great Principles Shared by All Religions*. New York, Fawcett Columbine.

Muller, Wayne (1992). *Legacy of the Heart*. New York, Fireside.

Peck, M. Scott (1978). *The Road Less Traveled*. New York, Simon & Schuster.

Wilson, Larry (1987). *Changing the Game: The New Way to Sell*. New York: Fireside.

123